SAINSBURY'S

CHOCOLATE COOKING

RHONA NEWMAN

ACKNOWLEDGEMENTS

Series Editor: **Nicola Hill**
Editor: **Mary-Clare Jerram**
Copy Editor: **Jeni Fleetwood**
Art Direction: **Sara Kidd**
Designer: **Accident**
Production Controllers: **Audrey Johnston and Janet Slater**
Photographer: **Paul Grater**
Home Economist: **Nichola Palmer**
Stylist: **Marian Price**
Jacket Photographer: **Vernon Morgan**
Jacket Home Economist: **Allyson Birch**
Jacket Stylist: **Lorrie Mack**

NOTES

1.   Standard level spoon measurements are used in all recipes.
1 tablespoon = one 15 ml spoon
1 teaspoon = one 5 ml spoon

2.   Both metric and imperial measurements have been given in all recipes. Use one set of measurements only and not a mixture of both.

3.   Ovens should be preheated to the specified temperature – if using a fan assisted oven, follow manufacturer's instructions for adjusting the temperature.

4.   Eggs should be size 3 unless otherwise stated.

5.   Milk should be full-fat unless otherwise stated.

6.   All microwave information is based on a 650 watt oven. Follow manufacturer's instructions for an oven with a different wattage.

Published exclusively for
J Sainsbury plc
Stamford Street, London SE1 9LL
by Cathay Books
Michelin House
81 Fulham Road, London SW3 6RB

First published 1989

© Cathay Books 1989
ISBN 0 86178 566 5

Produced by Mandarin Offset in Hong Kong
Printed and Bound in Hong Kong

CONTENTS

INTRODUCTION

REFINE THE ART OF CHOCOLATE COOKING, SO YOU CAN SATISFY THE DESIRES OF YOUR FRIENDS AND FAMILY FOR HOT AND COLD DESSERTS, ICE CREAMS, GÂTEAUX, BISCUITS AND SWEETS, FLAVOURED WITH THEIR FAVOURITE INDULGENCE.

Food of the gods – that's the translation of the botanical name for the plant that gives us chocolate – and very apt it is, too. For centuries the versatile bean of the cacao tree has provided untold pleasure as a beverage, a snack or sweet, a flavouring, or simply a decoration – an irresistible indulgence!

During the sixteenth century a bitter grainy drink made from the cocoa bean was popular among the Aztec Emperors of South America (the cacao tree grows in the tropical areas of Southern and Central America). Eventually the cocoa bean was taken to Spain, where the flavour of the drink was much improved by the addition of sugar. For a century this secret recipe was closely guarded. It was finally revealed in the seventeenth century – and the fashion for drinking chocolate spread swiftly across Europe. By 1650, Chocolate Houses had become important meeting places for the fashionable and wealthy in England.

It was not until the nineteenth century that chocolate was made into an edible bar. Since then it has become increasingly popular for cooking, eating and drinking, with some devotees becoming self-confessed chocoholics, unable to resist its lure! As a result of increased demand, the cocoa tree is now grown in the East Indies and West Indies as well as West Africa.

THE MAKING OF COCOA

All chocolate products are based upon cocoa in varying amounts. To meet an increasing demand for the products, manufacturing methods have been much improved.

Most of the cocoa beans used in Britain are imported from West Africa. Once removed from their pods, the beans are left to ferment and are then dried and roasted to obtain maximum flavour. The shell of the bean is removed leaving the kernel or nib. These nibs are ground to a thick dark paste called chocolate liquor. This is then passed between rollers which remove the fat or cocoa butter to leave a dry powdery mass which is ground into cocoa powder.

FLAVOURS

Drinking chocolate is cocoa combined with sugar, so that it dissolves readily; its prime use is for drinks. In cooking it has a milder flavour than cocoa. It is sometimes mixed with cocoa when used in cakes and desserts.

Malted chocolate is also intended for drinks, but gives a characteristic flavour when used in recipes. Its most common use is in teabreads to which it imparts a malt and chocolate flavour. The grains contain malt and sugar as well as cocoa.

TYPES

Eating and cooking chocolates are made from chocolate liquor which is blended with additional cocoa butter, sugar and flavourings such as vanilla. The more liquor and butter (cocoa solids) a chocolate contains, the better its quality.

COUVERTURE

This richly flavoured confectioner's chocolate has a high proportion of cocoa butter, which gives it a glossy appearance and a smooth but brittle texture. It has a strong, fine flavour and is more expensive than other types of chocolate. To melt and set successfully the chocolate must be heated and cooled to precise temperatures, which makes it difficult to use. This, coupled with its high cost, largely restricts its use to professional confec-tioners. It is not used in recipes in this book.

PLAIN OR BITTER CHOCOLATE

This category includes plain or dark chocolate with a minimum of 34 per cent cocoa solids, although the best results in cooking are obtained with a chocolate of 50 per cent minimum solids. (Sains-bury's sell a deluxe cooking chocolate with a minimum of 51 per cent cocoa solids). Plain or bitter chocolate is most commonly used in recipes. A slightly more bitter version, made from a more highly roasted cocoa bean and with very little sugar can replace part of the chocolate used in some recipes if a less sweet flavour is preferred.

MILK CHOCOLATE

This was originally made in 1875 by adding con-densed milk to the chocolate liquor. It contains less chocolate liquor than plain chocolate and is now made with the addition of dried milk. The flavour is milder than that of plain chocolate which makes it less suitable for cooking. Though used in milk puddings it lends itself more to decorations, top-pings and sauces. A deluxe milk cooking chocolate, with a minimum of 30 per cent cocoa solids and 20 per cent milks solids is sold by Sainsbury's.

WHITE CHOCOLATE

This is not true chocolate as it does not contain chocolate liquor. It is made from cocoa butter, milk and sugar. Due to the mild flavour, it is not really suitable for cooking apart from for its novelty value. Use it as a contrast to dark chocolate, for decoration, or to create a smooth sweet base as in an icing or ice cream.

CHOCOLATE FLAVOUR CAKE COVERING

This is much cheaper than plain chocolate but it lacks the intensity of flavour. It is either plain or milk flavoured and contains chocolate essences and added vegetable fat such as coconut or palm kernel oils instead of cocoa butter. It melts more readily than plain chocolate and when reset has a gloss lacking in most other forms of chocolate. This makes it particularly suitable for toppings, fillings, sauces and decoration, although it can be used for flavouring puddings and cakes.

DIABETIC CHOCOLATE

This is made in a similar way to plain or milk chocolate but is sweetened with sorbitol or fructose rather than sugar. It has a pleasant bittersweet flavour and can replace ordinary chocolate in any recipe. Contrary to common belief it is not lower in calories than other chocolate!

COCOA POWDER

Adding cocoa powder is the most economical way to achieve a good chocolate flavour in cakes, biscuits and other baking recipes. For the best results, the cocoa powder must be blended evenly into the mixture, either by sifting it with the other ingredients, or by mixing it with a little boiling water to form a smooth paste and then combining it with the rest of the ingredients.

If you use cocoa powder in an uncooked recipe – perhaps a cold dessert – it is vital you break down the starch cells first, through cooking: do this by blending it with a hot liquid, such as water or milk, before using it in the recipe.

CHOCOLATE ADDITIONS AND DECORATIONS

There are many chocolate products which can be used to enhance chocolate recipes or added as a decoration. These include chocolate drops (which do not melt when baked), buttons, flakes (which can be used whole, cut into shavings or crumbled), chocolate mini-logs, sweets, mint chocolates, chocolate biscuits, chocolate leaves, cups and shells.

BUYING AND STORING CHOCOLATE

If stored in a cool, dry place, cocoa powder should keep for up to 1 year. Chocolate bars and products should be stored in a cool, dry place and used by any stated 'best before' dates stamped on the wrapping. During hot weather chocolate may be kept in the refrigerator but it tends to lose some of its gloss. It should be wrapped well as it readily absorbs odours.

Sometimes a greyish white 'bloom' appears on chocolate. This is caused by exposure to varying temperatures which results in the cocoa butter and sugar crystals rising to the surface. This does not affect the flavour of the chocolate and will disappear on melting.

MELTING CHOCOLATE

Care is required when melting chocolate as it will become hard and granular if it is exposed to too much heat. Water or steam should not come into contact with melting chocolate as it will 'seize' (solidify). However, butter or oil may be added before or after melting without affecting the result.

SAUCEPAN METHOD

Place the broken chocolate in the top of a double boiler or a small heatproof bowl that will fit snugly over a saucepan. Place a small amount of water in the saucepan – the upper pan or bowl should not touch the water. Bring the water to the boil, remove the pan from the heat, then place the bowl or double boiler over the top. Stir occasionally to speed melting, but do not allow the chocolate to overheat or it will solidify.

If you add a liquid – water, milk, cream or a fruit juice – to the chocolate, you can melt it in a saucepan over direct heat. You should use a heavy-based saucepan, and add enough liquid to cover the base. Heat very gently until it is smooth, stirring occasionally. If you overheat the chocolate, and it becomes a solid mass, you can sometimes rectify the situation by beating in a little vegetable oil. The chocolate cannot then be used for icing or decorating cakes and gâteaux but it is suitable as a flavouring for desserts.

MICROWAVE METHOD
Place the broken chocolate in a microwave-proof bowl. To melt 75 g (3 oz) plain chocolate, cook on Full Power for 3 minutes, then stir well to melt completely.

Milk, white and cooking chocolate will take less time to melt. To avoid overheating, melt no more than 75-125 g (3-4 oz) chocolate at a time. Cook for an initial period of 2 minutes on Medium Power, then for further 1-minute periods until melted.

CHOCOLATE DECORATIONS
Chocolate makes an ideal decoration for many desserts and cakes, even if they are not chocolate-based. Some decorations are very simple to make while others need a little time and patience. It is worth making more than is required. Not only does this allow for breakages; it also provides a stockpile which may be stored in an airtight container in a cool place for several weeks. Chocolate decorations can be stored in the refrigerator if well wrapped, but they tend to lose their sheen. Plain or bitter chocolate gives the best results but chocolate flavour cake covering may also be used. White chocolate, when grated or made into curls, caraque or scrolls, provides a useful contrast to darker coloured chocolate in decoration.

CHOCOLATE CURLS
The chocolate should be at room temperature. Hold it over a plate and draw the blade of a vegetable peeler along the edge so that the curls fall on to the plate.

CHOCOLATE CARAQUE AND SCROLLS
Pour melted chocolate over a marble slab or cool work surface and spread to a thickness of 3 mm (1/8 inch). Leave to set for 30 minutes. To make short scrolls, place the edge of a metal spatula under the chocolate and push away from the body. Caraque or long scrolls are made by placing the blade of a long sharp knife on the surface of the chocolate. Using both hands, push the knife away from the body at an angle of 45°, rotating the handle in a quarter circle to scrape off a thin layer of chocolate.

CHOCOLATE TRIANGLES AND RECTANGLES
Pour melted chocolate on to a small baking sheet or into a shallow square tin lined with greaseproof or waxed paper. Spread to a thickness of 3 mm (1/8 inch) and leave to set for 30 minutes. Invert the chocolate on to a sheet of greaseproof or waxed paper and trim the edges with a sharp knife. Using a ruler, mark even-sized squares and cut out. Slice some in half, diagonally, to make triangles or cut them vertically to make rectangles.

CHOCOLATE DECORATIONS: CURLS, CARAQUE AND TRIANGLES

Making chocolate curls

Making chocolate caraque

Making chocolate triangles

MAKING CHOCOLATE ROSE LEAVES

Painting the leaves with chocolate   *Drying the chocolate leaf*   *Peeling away the leaf*

CHOPPED CHOCOLATE

The chocolate should be at room temperature. Place it on a board and chop roughly with a sharp heavy knife.

GRATED CHOCOLATE

Chill the chocolate for 15-20 minutes then grate with a grating disc of a food processor or hand grater. A rotary hand grater may also be used. If using a hand grater work over a large plate or sheet of greaseproof paper to catch all the bits. Hold the chocolate bar with a piece of foil to avoid it melting in the heat of the hand.

CHOCOLATE SHAPES

Pour melted chocolate on to greaseproof or waxed paper and spread to a thickness of 3 mm (1/8 inch). Allow to cool for about 30 minutes, but do not let it become too hard or the chocolate shapes will splinter.

Invert the chocolate on to a second piece of paper and use small biscuit, pastry or sweet cutters to make shapes. Any leftover chocolate may be melted and used again.

CHOCOLATE LEAVES

Fresh, non-poisonous leaves with distinct veins should be used, such as rose, bay or holly. These should be thoroughly washed and carefully dried. Melt the chocolate on a plate or in a wide heatproof bowl. Pull the underside of the leaves along the surface of the chocolate until coated or use a small paint brush to apply the chocolate. Leave the leaf coated side up to dry.

Carefully peel away the leaf, starting at the stem. Handle the chocolate leaves with care to prevent damaging them.

CHOCOLATE DIPPING

Fruit and nuts may be partially or wholly coated in chocolate and used as decorations or served as petit fours. Strawberries, grapes, segmented orange, pineapple, melon, dried apricots and dates are all suitable. Glacé fruits may also be used, but it is best to wash off sugar coatings and dry the fruit before dipping. Hazelnuts, whole or half walnuts, almonds and brazil nuts make good decorations or are just enjoyable to eat!

Melt the chocolate and use at body temperature (about 40°C, 90°F). Spear the pieces of fruit or nuts with a fine skewer and dip into the chocolate to completely or partially cover. Tap the skewer on the side of the dish to drain off any excess chocolate, then place the nuts and fruit on grease-proof or waxed paper to dry.

DRIZZLED CHOCOLATE

An extremely effective way to decorate cakes, biscuits and desserts is to drizzle melted chocolate flavour cake covering, Chocolate Glacé Icing (see page 91) or Chocolate Fudge Sauce (see page 92) over the top. Place the melted chocolate flavour cake covering, icing or sauce in a piping bag with a very small nozzle and drizzle it quickly over the surface. Alternatively use a metal teaspoon.

CHOCOLATE CASES

Making these takes a little more time than some of

the simpler decorations but they are very effective when filled with ice cream, mousse, or chocolate syllabub and topped with a nut or piece of fruit.

Place several paper cake cases inside each other to give a rigid shell. Use melted chocolate at an approximate temperature of 40°C, 90°F and spoon or brush the inside of the cases to coat. Leave to set for several hours then add a second layer of chocolate to the first. Leave to set and refrigerate until required. Apply the second chocolate layer at least 6 hours before using the cases. Peel off the paper very gently and use the cases as required, handling them carefully.

ACCOMPANIMENTS

As chocolate recipes can be very rich many in this book suggest the use of fromage frais or Greek yogurt as an accompaniment or replacement for cream. Both of these products are considerably lower in fat than cream and make a refreshing contrast to the chocolate.

Other suitable accompaniments for chocolate dishes are sauces (see page 92) or biscuits, either baked yourself or bought.

CAROB

This is not chocolate, but a popular alternative. It is made from the fruit of a Mediterranean evergreen tree which bears flat, dark brown pods about the size of a banana. These contain small black seeds so uniform in size that the word 'carat' as a measure of weight derived from them. This measure is used today, 4 carob beans being the equivalent to 1 carat of gold in weight.

Carob powder or flour is made by grinding the seeds. It has a lower fat content than cocoa, contains more natural sugar, is free of stimulants, contains B vitamins and some minerals. However, connoisseurs say that it can never match the flavour and texture of good chocolate!

Carob powder can replace cocoa powder in recipes. It may be used weight for weight, but avoid adding it in large quantities as it will impart a bitter flavour. Because of the natural sugar content in carob, the sugar in the recipe may be reduced slightly. Do not be put off by the light brown colour of carob; once cooked, it gives a very dark finish to cakes, biscuits and puddings. It is also made into bars similar to slabs of chocolate which may be melted for toppings, decorations and sauces.

TO ASSEMBLE A SWISS ROLL

While baking the sponge (see Mocha Swiss Roll, page 59), place a piece of greaseproof paper, more than 30 × 20 cm (12 × 8 inches) in size, on a dampened tea towel laid on a flat working surface. Dust this with caster sugar.

Remove the cooked sponge from the oven, turn it out on to the greaseproof paper, and peel away the lining paper. Trim the edges with a long sharp knife and, along one short side about 1 cm (½ inch) from the edge, make a dent. Gently roll up the sponge, keeping the greaseproof paper inside. Transfer to a wire rack, cover with the damp tea towel, and leave to cool.

When the sponge is completely cold, carefully unroll it and, using a palette knife, spread the icing. Roll up the sponge again, fairly tightly.

THE FINAL STAGES OF MAKING A SWISS ROLL

Turning out the sponge

Rolling up the sponge

Spreading the buttercream icing

QUICK DESSERTS

MAKE THESE QUICK, SIMPLE DESSERTS FOR EVERYDAY MEALS AND EMERGENCY ENTERTAINING, USING ANY CONVENIENCE FOODS YOU HAVE AT HAND AND BASIC STORE-CUPBOARD INGREDIENTS — EGGS, NUTS, RAISINS, SUGAR AND, OF COURSE, THE INEVITABLE CHOCOLATE.

BANANA CHOCOLATE SNOW

3 large bananas
2 teaspoons lemon juice
75 g (3 oz) plain chocolate, melted
2 egg whites
TO DECORATE:
White Chocolate Curls (see page 7)
1 lemon slice, quartered

Mash the bananas in a bowl and stir in the melted chocolate until it is all well mixed.

In a bowl, whisk the egg whites until stiff and fold into the banana mixture. Spoon into individual serving dishes and decorate with white chocolate curls and lemon. Serve immediately.

SERVES 4

Nutritional content per serving: Carbohydrate: 31 g   Fat: 7 g   Fibre: 3 g   Kilocalories: 194

CHOCOLATE GRAPE BRULÉE

PREPARE THIS DESSERT A FEW HOURS IN ADVANCE OF SERVING, TO CHILL IT THOROUGHLY BEFORE BEING GRILLED. THE ESSENCE OF THIS BRULÉE IS THE CONTRAST BETWEEN THE COOL GRAPES AND THE HOT TOPPING OF CHOCOLATE, SUGAR AND NUTS

250 g (8 oz) white seedless grapes
2 × 142 ml (5 fl oz) cartons soured cream
50 g (2 oz) plain chocolate, melted
4 teaspoons soft brown sugar
4 teaspoons chopped nuts

Divide the grapes between 4 ramekins or small heatproof dishes. Place the soured cream in a bowl and stir until smooth. Add the melted chocolate, swirling it into the mixture to give a marbled effect. Spoon the marbled cream over the grapes and chill in the refrigerator for at least 1 hour.

Just before serving, sprinkle with the sugar and nuts and place under a preheated grill for 3-5 minutes until the nuts have browned and the sugar has melted. Serve immediately.

SERVES 4

Nutritional content per serving: Carbohydrate: 25 g   Fat: 21 g   Fibre: 1 g   Kilocalories: 301

CHOCOLATE FRUIT SALAD

1 large orange, separated into segments
1 dessert apple, cored and sliced
125 g (4 oz) seedless white grapes
½ charentais or cantaloupe melon, diced
2 tablespoons sherry
2 tablespoons lemon juice
175 g (6 oz) plain chocolate, melted
single cream to serve (optional)

Arrange the fruit carefully in a shallow dish and spoon the sherry and lemon juice over. Cover and set aside for 1 hour to soak.

Spearing a piece of fruit on a skewer, dip it into the melted chocolate to coat up to half of each piece. Place on a sheet of waxed or greaseproof paper to dry at room temperature. Repeat with the remaining fruit.

Arrange on flat dishes and serve immediately, with single cream if using.

SERVES 4

Nutritional content per serving: Carbohydrate: 44 g   Fat: 13 g   Fibre: 3 g   Kilocalories: 300

Chocolate Grape Brulée; Banana Chocolate Snow; Chocolate Fruit Salad

POTS AU CHOCOLAT

finely grated rind of ½ orange
3 eggs, separated
65 ml (2½ fl oz) single cream
125 g (4 oz) plain chocolate, melted
1 tablespoon Cointreau or orange juice
TO DECORATE:
65 ml (2½ fl oz) whipping cream, whipped
grated chocolate

Add the orange rind, egg yolks and single cream to the bowl of melted chocolate and mix well. Stir in the Cointreau or orange juice. Whisk the egg whites until stiff and fold into the chocolate mixture.

Spoon into 4-6 small dishes and refrigerate until set. To serve, decorate with whipped cream and grated chocolate.

Freezing: is recommended before decorating. When set cover with foil and seal in a freezer bag. These will freeze for up to 6 weeks. Defrost in the refrigerator for 3-4 hours.

SERVES 4-6

Nutritional content per serving:	Carbohydrate: 22 g	Fat: 23 g	Fibre: 0.5 g	Kilocalories: 315

CHOCOLATE MOUSSE LAYER

3 × 62.5 g (2½ oz) cartons chocolate
  mousse
50 g (2 oz) plain chocolate, chopped
2 kiwi fruit
4 tablespoons crunchy oat cereal
2 × 150 g (5.2 oz) cartons apricot and
  mango thick and creamy yogurt

Place the mousses in a bowl and stir in most of the chocolate, reserving a little for decoration. Chop the kiwi fruit, keeping some to slice for decoration.

Spoon the crunchy oat cereal into the base of 4 tall sundae glasses. Add, in layers, the yogurt, chopped kiwi fruit and chocolate mousse mixture, ending with a layer of yogurt.

Slice the reserved kiwi fruit and use to decorate the desserts with the reserved chocolate. Serve chilled.

SERVES 4

Nutritional content per serving:	Carbohydrate: 46 g	Fat: 10 g	Fibre: 2 g	Kilocalories: 296

CHOC TOP MERINGUES

4 meringue nests
4 tablespoons whipped cream or natural
  fromage frais
4 scoops Chocolate Ice Cream
  (see page 42)
4 strawberries, halved

Place the meringue nests on individual small plates and spoon 1 tablespoon of cream or fromage frais into each nest. Top each nest with one scoop of the chocolate ice cream.

Decorate the top of each meringue dessert with the strawberry halves. Serve immediately.

SERVES 4

Nutritional content per serving:	Carbohydrate: 73 g	Fat: 22 g	Fibre: 0.5 g	Kilocalories: 507

Pots au Chocolat; Choc Top Meringues; Chocolate Mousse Layer

CHOCOLATE RASPBERRY RIPPLE

250 g (8 oz) raspberries
75 g (3 oz) plain chocolate, melted
250 g (8 oz) natural fromage frais
65 ml (2½ fl oz) whipping cream, whipped
mint leaves to decorate

Set aside a few raspberries for decoration. Cook the rest over a low heat until soft. Mix with the chocolate and allow to cool.

In a mixing bowl, beat the fromage frais with the cream until thoroughly blended. Add the chocolate and raspberry mixture and stir lightly to create a marbled effect. Spoon into 4 dishes and chill. Decorate with raspberries and mint leaves.

Microwave: Place the raspberries in a shallow bowl, cover lightly and cook on Full Power for 1-2 minutes.

SERVES 4

Nutritional content per serving: Carbohydrate: 17 g   Fat: 11 g   Fibre: 5 g   Kilocalories: 208

CHOCOLATE BRANDY SYLLABUB

3 tablespoons drinking chocolate
2 tablespoons brandy
1 tablespoon water
2 tablespoons chocolate yogurt
1 × 284 ml (10 fl oz) carton whipping
  cream, whipped
1 egg white
TO DECORATE:
4 teaspoons chopped hazelnuts, toasted
Chocolate Curls (see page 7)

In a bowl, combine the drinking chocolate with the brandy and water, then stir in the yogurt and mix well. Fold into the bowl of whipped cream.

Whisk the egg white until stiff and fold into the chocolate cream. Spoon into 4 small glass stem dishes and chill. Top with the hazelnuts and chocolate curls and serve with wafer curls.

SERVES 4

Nutritional content per serving: Carbohydrate: 15 g   Fat: 29 g   Fibre: 0.5 g   Kilocalories: 346

STUFFED PEARS

2 × 411 g (14½ oz) cans pear halves in
  natural juice, drained
75 g (3 oz) plain chocolate, broken
25 g (1 oz) butter
50 g (2 oz) muesli
25 g (1 oz) chopped mixed nuts

Place 2 pear halves, cut side up, on each of 4 serving plates. Slice the remaining pears and arrange on the serving plates.

Place the chocolate and butter in a heatproof bowl over a pan of gently simmering water. Stir until the chocolate has melted, then add the muesli and nuts and mix well. Spoon the mixture into the centre of the pears. Serve cold with cream or natural yogurt.

Microwave: To melt the chocolate and the butter, cook in a bowl on Full Power for 2½ minutes.

SERVES 4

Nutritional content per serving: Carbohydrate: 30 g   Fat: 15 g   Fibre: 5 g   Kilocalories: 263

Chocolate Brandy Syllabub; Chocolate Raspberry Ripple; Stuffed Pears

CHOCOLATE RAISIN FOOL

50 g (2 oz) raisins
2 tablespoons sherry
1 tablespoon custard powder
1 tablespoon drinking chocolate
2 teaspoons cocoa powder
1 tablespoon caster sugar
300 ml (½ pint) milk
1 × 142 ml (5 fl oz) carton whipping cream, whipped
small chocolate flakes, halved, to decorate

Place the raisins in a bowl and add the sherry. Leave them to soak for about 1-2 hours.

In a bowl, mix the custard powder, drinking chocolate, cocoa powder and sugar to a paste with a little of the milk. Place the remaining milk in a saucepan and bring to the boil. Pour on to the chocolate mixture, stirring constantly. Return to the pan and heat, stirring until the custard thickens. Cook for 1 minute. Place the pan in a bowl of water to cool, stirring the custard frequently.

Fold the whipped cream and the custard into the raisins and the sherry. Spoon into 4 individual dishes and decorate with the small chocolate flakes. Keep cool but do not refrigerate.

Microwave: Mix the custard powder, drinking chocolate, cocoa powder, sugar and milk in a microwave container. Cook on Full Power for 4 minutes, stirring after 2 minutes.

SERVES 4

Nutritional content per serving:	Carbohydrate: 26 g	Fat: 18 g	Fibre: 1 g	Kilocalories: 282

LEMON AND CHOCOLATE CRUNCH

75 g (3 oz) chocolate digestive biscuits, crushed
25 g (1 oz) hazelnuts, toasted and roughly chopped
1 × 227 g (8 oz) carton skimmed milk soft cheese or curd cheese
250 g (8 oz) natural fromage frais
50 g (2 oz) caster sugar
finely grated rind of 1 lemon
4 tablespoons lemon juice
50 g (2 oz) chocolate, grated
TO DECORATE:
1 lemon slice, quartered
Chocolate Curls (see page 7)

In a small bowl, combine the crushed biscuits and toasted hazelnuts and mix well.

Place the cheese, fromage frais, sugar, lemon rind and lemon juice in a mixing bowl and beat until well blended. Stir in the grated chocolate.

Layer both the mixtures in 4 tall stem glasses, starting and finishing with the chocolate lemon cream. Chill until required. To serve, decorate each portion with lemon and chocolate curls.

SERVES 4

Nutritional content per serving:	Carbohydrate: 43 g	Fat: 14 g	Fibre: 2 g	Kilocalories: 368

Chocolate Raisin Fool; Lemon and Chocolate Crunch; Chocolate Fondue

CHOCOLATE FONDUE

1 × 100 g (3½ oz) bar Toblerone chocolate
50 g (2 oz) plain chocolate
2 tablespoons double cream
1 tablespoon rum
TO SERVE:
selection of fruit including strawberries, raspberries, cherries, sliced banana
sponge fingers or langues de chats

Break the Toblerone and plain chocolate into a heatproof bowl and add the cream. Place over a saucepan of gently simmering water. Stir until the chocolate has melted. Stir in the rum and continue to heat, stirring for 1 minute.

Pour the sauce into a warmed heatproof bowl. Serve with a selection of fruits and biscuits for dipping, using bamboo skewers to spear the fruit.

Microwave: Place both the chocolates and double cream in a bowl and cook on Medium Power for 2-3 minutes, stirring once or twice. Stir in the rum and serve.

SERVES 4

Nutritional content per serving:	Carbohydrate: 23 g	Fat: 15 g	Fibre: 0.5 g	Kilocalories: 240

CHOCOLATE FRUIT PIZZA

2 quantities (250 g/8 oz) shortcrust pastry
   (see Chocolate-Coated Tarts, page 64),
   chilled
15 g (½ oz) caster sugar
2 × 62.5 g (2½ oz) cartons chocolate
   mousse
250 g (8 oz) fresh fruit, such as kiwi fruit,
   strawberries, grapes or peaches, sliced or
   halved
25 g (1 oz) white chocolate, grated

Roll out the pastry to a circle 20 cm (8 inches) in diameter and place on a baking sheet. Pinch the edges to make a rim and sprinkle with the sugar. Bake in a preheated oven, 190°C, 375°F, Gas Mark 5 for 15-20 minutes. Transfer to a wire rack to cool.

Mix the mousses in a bowl, then spread over the pastry. Arrange the fruit over the mousse topping. Decorate with the grated white chocolate and serve.

SERVES 4

Nutritional content per serving: Carbohydrate: 47 g   Fat: 16 g   Fibre: 2 g   Kilocalories: 345

CHOCOLATE NUT CREAMS

40 g (1 ½ oz) chopped mixed nuts
40 g (1 ½ oz) medium oatmeal
75 g (3 oz) plain chocolate, melted
1 tablespoon whisky (optional)
1 × 150 g (5.2 oz) carton natural yogurt
1 × 142 ml (5 fl oz) carton whipping cream, whipped
chopped nuts, toasted, to decorate

In a small bowl, mix the nuts and oatmeal. Spread the mixture over a baking sheet and place under a preheated grill for 2-3 minutes, stirring frequently until evenly browned. Set aside to cool.

Mix the melted chocolate with the whisky, if using. Add the yogurt and then the prepared nut mixture. Stir well, then fold in the whipped cream. Spoon into 4 individual dishes. Chill until required. To serve, decorate with toasted nuts.

Microwave: Heat the nuts and oatmeal in a microwave container on Full Power for 5 minutes, stirring twice.

SERVES 4

Nutritional content per serving: Carbohydrate: 26 g   Fat: 26 g   Fibre: 2 g   Kilocalories: 367

CHOCOLATE BANANA SWIRL

SERVE THIS TREAT WITH WAFERS, CHOCOLATE SHORTBREAD (SEE PAGE 78) OR CHOCOLATE VIENNESE BISCUITS (SEE PAGE 76)

25 g (1 oz) cornflour
15 g (½ oz) cocoa powder
300 ml (½ pint) milk
25 g (1 oz) soft brown sugar
1 large ripe banana, mashed
2 tablespoons natural fromage frais
2 tablespoons natural yogurt

In a bowl, mix the cornflour and cocoa powder to a paste with a little of the milk. Stir in the brown sugar. Place the remaining milk in a saucepan and bring to the boil. Pour on to the chocolate mixture, stirring constantly. Return to the pan and heat, stirring until the custard thickens. Cook for 1 minute. Place the pan in a bowl of water to cool, stirring the custard frequently. When cool, add the mashed banana and mix well.

In a small bowl, mix the fromage frais with the yogurt. Swirl into the chocolate mixture to give a marbled effect. Spoon into a serving dish and chill until required. Serve with wafers.

Microwave: In a bowl, combine the cornflour, cocoa powder, milk and brown sugar. Mix well and cook on Full Power for 4 minutes, stirring after 2 minutes.

SERVES 4

Nutritional content per serving: Carbohydrate: 25 g   Fat: 5 g   Fibre: 1 g   Kilocalories: 163

Chocolate Nut Creams; Chocolate Fruit Pizza; Chocolate Banana Swirl

Desserts

Traditional favourites — trifles, tarts, soufflés, sponge puddings, pancakes, and meringue pies — become even more tempting when flavoured with chocolate. Try out some of these imaginative, but delicious, variations on an old theme.

HOT CHOCOLATE TRIFLE

QUICK, EASY AND POPULAR WITH CHILDREN, THIS TRIFLE MAY ALSO BE MADE USING CANNED PEARS, PEACHES OR MANDARIN ORANGES

1 x 411 g (14½ oz) can apricot halves in
    fruit juice
1 chocolate Swiss roll, sliced
2 tablespoons custard powder
2 eggs, separated
1 tablespoon drinking chocolate
1 teaspoon cocoa powder
2 teaspoons granulated sugar
600 ml (1 pint) milk
125 g (4 oz) caster sugar

Drain the apricots, reserving the juice. Arrange the Swiss roll slices and apricot halves on the base of a 1.2 litre (2 pint) ovenproof dish. Spoon some of the reserved fruit juice over the top.

In a bowl, mix the custard powder, egg yolks, drinking chocolate, cocoa powder and sugar to a paste with a little of the milk. Place the remaining milk in a saucepan and heat until almost boiling. Add to the custard mixture, stirring constantly and return to the pan. Heat, stirring, for 1 minute until thick. Pour over the apricot mixture.

In a clean bowl, whisk the egg whites until stiff. Whisk in half the sugar, then fold in the remainder. Spoon or pipe the meringue over the custard, then bake in a preheated oven, 180°C, 350°F, Gas Mark 4 for 20 minutes or until the meringue is golden. Serve hot or warm.

SERVES 4-6

Nutritional content per serving: Carbohydrate: 103 g   Fat: 15 g   Fibre: 2 g   Kilocalories: 568

CHOCOLATE BAKEWELL TART

125 g (4 oz) plain flour
pinch of salt
25 g (1 oz) margarine
25 g (1 oz) lard
1 tablespoon water
FILLING:
3 tablespoons apricot jam
50 g (2 oz) butter, softened
50 g (2 oz) caster sugar
1 egg
50 g (2 oz) ground almonds
25 g (1 oz) plain flour
½ teaspoon baking powder
2 tablespoons cocoa powder
1 tablespoon milk
2–3 drops almond flavouring
1 tablespoon flaked almonds

Sift the flour and salt into a mixing bowl. Rub in the margarine and lard until the mixture resembles fine breadcrumbs, then add the water and mix to a stiff dough. Turn on to a floured surface and knead until smooth. Roll out to line an 18 cm (7 inch) flan tin or dish. Prick the base and spread evenly with the apricot jam. Set aside.

In a bowl, cream the butter with the sugar until pale and fluffy. Beat in the egg, then fold in the ground almonds. Sift together the flour, baking powder and cocoa powder then fold into the mixture with the milk and almond flavouring. Spoon the mixture over the jam in the pastry case and level the top. Sprinkle with the flaked almonds.

Place on a baking sheet and bake in a preheated oven, 190°C, 375°F, Gas Mark 5 for 35-40 minutes or until firm, covering with foil if the top becomes too crisp. Serve hot or cold with Chocolate Custard Sauce (see page 92) or cream in a jug.

SERVES 4-6

Nutritional content per serving: Carbohydrate: 53 g   Fat: 34 g   Fibre: 3 g   Kilocalories: 539

Hot Chocolate Trifle; Chocolate Bakewell Tart

CHOCOLATE BREAD AND BUTTER PUDDING

6 slices white bread, crusts removed
40 g (1½ oz) butter
40 g (1½ oz) chocolate and hazelnut spread
600 ml (1 pint) milk
25 g (1 oz) drinking chocolate
25 g (1 oz) caster sugar
2 eggs
50 g (2 oz) sultanas
grated chocolate

Spread the bread with the butter and chocolate and hazelnut spread. Cut into squares or triangles and arrange in a greased 1.2 litre (2 pint) ovenproof dish.

Heat about a third of the milk in a saucepan, then whisk in the drinking chocolate and sugar. Allow to cool. Beat the eggs with the remaining milk and stir in the chocolate milk.

Sprinkle the sultanas over the bread, then strain the milk over the top. Leave to stand for 30 minutes. Bake in a preheated oven, 160°C, 325°F, Gas Mark 3 for 45 minutes-1 hour or until the pudding is set and crisp on top. Serve immediately, sprinkled with grated chocolate.

SERVES 4

Nutritional content per serving: Carbohydrate: 49 g   Fat: 16 g   Fibre: 2 g   Kilocalories: 378

Chocolate Bread and Butter Pudding

Hot Chocolate Soufflé

HOT CHOCOLATE SOUFFLÉ

50 g (2 oz) butter
50 g (2 oz) plain flour
300 ml (½ pint) warm milk
75 g (3 oz) plain chocolate, melted
40 g (1½ oz) caster sugar
1 tablespoon brandy or sherry
3 egg yolks
4 egg whites

Melt the butter in a saucepan, then stir in the flour and cook for 1 minute. Remove from the heat. Mix the milk and melted chocolate together, then gradually stir into the butter and flour, mixing well after each addition. Return to the heat and cook, stirring, for 2 minutes. Allow to cool slightly, then beat in the caster sugar, brandy or sherry and egg yolks.

In a deep bowl, whisk the egg whites until stiff. Fold a little of the beaten egg white into the chocolate mixture to lighten it, then carefully fold in the remainder.

Spoon into a greased 1.2 litre (2 pint) soufflé dish and bake in a preheated oven, 180°C, 350°F, Gas Mark 4 for 35-40 minutes or until well risen. Serve immediately, with single cream.

SERVES 4-6

Nutritional content per serving: Carbohydrate: 36 g   Fat: 25 g   Fibre: 1 g   Kilocalories: 412

Apricot and Prune Tart; Chocolate Apple Envelopes; Orange Black Magic Pudding

ORANGE BLACK MAGIC PUDDING

DURING BAKING, THIS PUDDING SEPARATES INTO A MOIST SPONGE ON TOP WITH AN ORANGE CUSTARD AT THE BOTTOM

50 g (2 oz) sunflower margarine
50 g (2 oz) soft brown sugar
50 g (2 oz) caster sugar
grated rind of 1 orange
2 eggs, separated
50 g (2 oz) self-raising flour
15 g (½ oz) cocoa powder
300 ml (½ pint) milk
juice of 1 orange, strained
icing sugar to dust

Beat together the margarine, brown sugar, caster sugar and orange rind in a mixing bowl until light and fluffy. Add the egg yolks and beat well.

Sift the flour and cocoa powder together, then fold into the mixture with the milk and orange juice.

In a separate bowl, whisk the egg whites until stiff and fold into the mixture. Spoon into a greased 1.2 litre (2 pint) ovenproof dish, placing this in a roasting tin half filled with water. Bake in a preheated oven, 200°C, 400°F, Gas Mark 6 for 45-50 minutes or until risen and firm on top. Dust with icing sugar. Serve hot with single cream or natural yogurt.

SERVES 4

Nutritional content per serving: Carbohydrate: 41 g   Fat: 17 g   Fibre: 0.5 g   Kilocalories: 338

APRICOT AND PRUNE TART

165 g (5½ oz) plain flour
1 tablespoon cocoa powder
1 tablespoon drinking chocolate
40 g (1½ oz) margarine
40 g (1½ oz) lard
1½ tablespoons water
grated chocolate to decorate
FILLING:
75 g (3 oz) dried prunes, soaked overnight
75 g (3 oz) dried apricots, soaked overnight
2 eggs
200 ml (7 fl oz) natural yogurt
25 g (1 oz) soft brown sugar

Sift the flour, cocoa powder and drinking chocolate into a mixing bowl. Rub in the margarine and lard until the mixture resembles fine breadcrumbs. Add the water and mix to a firm dough. Turn on to a floured surface and knead until smooth. Wrap in foil and chill in the refrigerator for 15 minutes.

Turn the dough on to a lightly floured surface and roll out to line a 23 cm (9 inch) flan tin or dish, then prick the base.

Make the filling. Drain the prunes and apricots. Remove the stones from the prunes and chop both fruits, then place in the flan case. In a bowl beat the eggs with the yogurt and sugar, then pour over the fruit. Bake in a preheated oven, 190°C, 375°F, Gas Mark 5 for 30-40 minutes or until the filling is set. Serve warm, sprinkled with grated chocolate and accompanied by Chocolate Sauce (see page 92) or single cream.

Freezing: is recommended. When cold wrap with tin foil and seal the tart in a freezer bag. It will keep for up to 4 months. Defrost in the refrigerator for 4 hours, then place in a preheated oven, 180°C, 350°F, Gas Mark 4 for 15-20 minutes. Towards the end of cooking, cover with foil to prevent browning.

SERVES 6-8

Nutritional content per serving:	Carbohydrate: 65 g	Fat: 25 g	Fibre: 9 g	Kilocalories: 514

CHOCOLATE APPLE ENVELOPES

50 g (2 oz) plain flour
40 g (1½ oz) wholemeal flour
25 g (1 oz) drinking chocolate
pinch of salt
1 egg, beaten
300 ml (½ pint) milk
FILLING:
1 kg (2 lb) Bramley cooking apples, peeled, cored and sliced
grated rind and juice of 1 orange
50 g (2 oz) granulated or caster sugar
1 tablespoon orange-flavoured liqueur
TO DECORATE:
White Chocolate Curls (see page 7)
fine strands of orange rind

Place the plain flour, wholemeal flour, drinking chocolate and salt in a bowl and make a well in the centre. Add the egg and half the milk. Beat until smooth, then gradually stir in the remaining milk. Pour this batter into a jug. Make 8 pancakes as described in the recipe for Banana and Chocolate Pancakes (see page 29). As each pancake is cooked, place it on a plate over a saucepan of gently simmering water to keep warm. Place a sheet of greaseproof paper between each pancake to prevent sticking, then cover with a lid.

To make the filling, place the apples in a saucepan with the orange rind and juice and sugar. Heat gently for 15 minutes, until the apples are soft. Cool slightly, add the liqueur and beat to a pulp.

Divide the mixture between the warm pancakes, fold each into 4 and arrange on a serving plate. Decorate with white chocolate curls and orange rind. Serve with cream or natural yogurt.

SERVES 4

Nutritional content per serving:	Carbohydrate: 63 g	Fat: 7 g	Fibre: 6 g	Kilocalories: 333

Semolina chocolate soufflé

600 ml (1 pint) milk
50 g (2 oz) plain chocolate, broken
3 tablespoons semolina
1–2 tablespoons caster sugar
1 egg, separated
grated nutmeg

Place the milk and chocolate in a saucepan and heat, stirring until the chocolate melts. Bring to the boil, then sprinkle the semolina over the milk. Lower the heat and cook slowly, stirring until the mixture comes to the boil and thickens. Stir in the sugar and simmer for 2 minutes more. Cool slightly then beat in the egg yolk.

Whisk the egg white until stiff, then fold into the mixture, mixing well. Spoon the semolina mixture into a greased 900 ml (1 ½ pint) soufflé dish and sprinkle with grated nutmeg. Bake in a preheated oven, 180°C, 350°F, Gas Mark 4 for 20 minutes until risen. Serve hot.

SERVES 4

Nutritional content per serving: Carbohydrate: 32 g   Fat: 13 g   Fibre: 1 g   Kilocalories: 269

French pear flan

125 g (4 oz) plain flour
20 g (¾ oz) cocoa powder
pinch of salt
50 g (2 oz) block margarine, cut into pieces
50 g (2 oz) caster sugar
2 egg yolks
2 drops vanilla flavouring
FILLING:
5 dessert pears
1 tablespoon water
1 ripe banana, mashed
1 tablespoon icing sugar (optional)
GLAZE:
3 tablespoons apricot jam
1 teaspoon lemon juice

Sift the flour, cocoa powder and salt on to a pastry board and make a well in the centre. Place the margarine, caster sugar, egg yolks and vanilla in the well. Using the fingertips of one hand work the fat, sugar and yolks together, then quickly draw in the flour and knead lightly until smooth. Wrap in foil and chill for 1 hour.

Place the dough on a lightly floured surface and roll out to line a 20 cm (8 inch) flan tin or dish. Prick the base and bake blind (lined with greaseproof paper and baking beans) in a preheated oven, 190°C, 375°F, Gas Mark 5 for 15 minutes. Remove the lining and return the pastry case to the oven for 5 minutes more. Set aside.

Peel, core and slice 3 pears and heat gently in a saucepan with the water until soft. Purée in a blender or food processor, then stir in the banana with icing sugar to taste. Spoon into the pastry case. Peel, core and slice the remaining pears and arrange over the purée. Return to the oven and bake for 25 minutes.

Make the glaze. Place the apricot jam and lemon juice in a saucepan. Bring to the boil over gentle heat, then strain through a sieve into a clean pan. Boil until clear. Brush the glaze over the pears and allow the flan to cool. Serve with cream or Greek yogurt.

Freezing: is recommended. When cold wrap with tin foil and seal in a freezer bag. This will keep for up to 4 months. Defrost at room temperature for 3 hours.

SERVES 6

Nutritional content per serving: Carbohydrate: 69 g   Fat: 16 g   Fibre: 5 g   Kilocalories: 428

French Pear Flan; Semolina Chocolate Soufflé

ORANGE AND BANANA PUDDING

125 g (4 oz) sunflower margarine
125 g (4 oz) caster sugar
2 eggs
125 g (4 oz) self-raising flour, sifted
15 g (½ oz) cocoa powder, sifted
grated rind and juice of ½ orange
2 ripe bananas, peeled and sliced
TO DECORATE:
1 ripe banana, sliced and sprinkled with
  lemon juice
fine strands of orange rind

Combine all the pudding ingredients except the bananas in a bowl and beat well for 3 minutes. Fold in the banana slices, then spoon the mixture into a greased 900 ml (1 ½ pint) pudding basin. Cover with greaseproof paper and tie securely.

Steam for 2 hours, topping up the steamer with water whenever necessary. Turn on to a serving plate and decorate with banana slices and fine strands of orange rind. Serve with Chocolate Custard Sauce (see page 92).

Microwave: Cook the pudding on Full Power for 4 minutes, turning halfway through. Allow to stand for 4-5 minutes.

SERVES 6

Nutritional content per serving: Carbohydrate: 45 g   Fat: 19 g   Fibre: 2 g   Kilocalories: 363

Orange and Banana Pudding

Banana and Chocolate Pancakes

BANANA AND CHOCOLATE PANCAKES

125 g (4 oz) plain flour
pinch of salt
1 egg, beaten
300 ml (½ pint) milk
FILLING:
2 large bananas
1 × 113 g (4 oz) carton skimmed milk soft cheese or curd cheese
1 × 125 g (4.4 oz) carton chocolate yogurt
1 banana, sliced diagonally, to decorate
Chocolate Fudge Sauce (see page 92) to serve

Sift the flour and salt into a mixing bowl and make a well in the centre. Add the egg and half the milk. Beat until smooth, then gradually stir in the remaining milk. Pour into a jug. Wipe an 18 cm (7 inch) non-stick frying pan with oil and place over a moderate heat for 30 seconds. Coat the base with a little batter and cook until the underside is lightly browned. Turn the pancake and cook the other side. Repeat, to make 8 pancakes. Cool on a wire rack.

Make the filling. Place the bananas in a bowl and mash well. Stir in the cheese and chocolate yogurt. Mix well, then divide the mixture between the pancakes. Roll up and arrange 2 on each individual dish decorated with banana slices. Pour a little of the chocolate fudge sauce over and serve the remainder separately.

Freezing: is recommended for the pancakes before filling. When cold stack them, interleaved with greaseproof paper. Wrap with tin foil and seal in a freezer bag. They will keep for up to 4 months. Defrost at room temperature for 1-2 hours and fill as above.

SERVES 4

Nutritional content per serving: Carbohydrate: 46 g   Fat: 5 g   Fibre: 3 g   Kilocalories: 273

Chocolate Pineapple Princess; Chocolate Ginger Profiteroles; Chocolate Jelly Mould

CHOCOLATE PINEAPPLE PRINCESS

600 ml (1 pint) milk
75 g (3 oz) plain chocolate, broken
15 g (½ oz) butter
125 g (4 oz) fresh breadcrumbs
2 eggs, separated
1 × 227 g (8 oz) can pineapple pieces in
   natural juice, drained
125 g (4 oz) caster sugar
caster sugar for dredging (optional)

Combine the milk, chocolate and butter in a saucepan. Heat until the chocolate has melted and the milk is almost boiling. Remove from the heat and stir in the breadcrumbs. Leave to stand for 10–15 minutes, then beat in the egg yolks.

Arrange the pineapple on the base of a 1.2 litre (2 pint) ovenproof dish, then pour the crumb mixture over the top. Bake in a preheated oven, 160°C, 325°F, Gas Mark 3 for 40 minutes or until set.

In a deep bowl, whisk the egg whites until stiff. Whisk in half the sugar, then fold in the remainder. Spoon or pipe the meringue over the pudding. Dredge with extra caster sugar, if using, and return to the oven for 20-25 minutes until the meringue is crisp and golden. Serve with whipped cream, natural yogurt or natural fromage frais.

SERVES 4

Nutritional content per serving: Carbohydrate: 73 g   Fat: 18 g   Fibre: 1 g   Kilocalories: 479

CHOCOLATE GINGER PROFITEROLES

65 g (2½ oz) plain flour
pinch of salt
50 g (2 oz) butter or margarine
150 ml (¼ pint) water
2 eggs, lightly beaten
FILLING:
1 × 142 ml (5 fl oz) carton double cream,
    whipped
2 tablespoons natural fromage frais
2 pieces stem ginger, chopped
2 teaspoons syrup from the stem ginger jar
Chocolate Fudge Sauce (see page 92)
    to serve

Sift the flour and salt twice on to a sheet of greaseproof paper. Place the butter or margarine and water in a saucepan and bring to the boil. As the liquid rises in the pan, remove from the heat and immediately shoot in all the flour. Beat well until the mixture forms a smooth ball, leaving the sides of the pan clean. Set the pan aside to cool slightly, then add the beaten eggs a little at a time, beating well.

Using a piping bag fitted with 1.5 cm (¾ inch) plain nozzle, pipe 20 small bun shapes on to greased baking sheets, allowing space for expansion. Bake in a preheated oven, 220°C, 425°F, Gas Mark 7 for 10 minutes, then lower the temperature to 190°C, 375°F, Gas Mark 5 and bake for 15-20 minutes or until golden. Make a slit in each bun to release the steam, then cool on a wire rack.

Make the filling. In a bowl, mix the whipped double cream and fromage frais. Stir in the stem ginger and syrup and mix well. Partially split the choux buns and pipe or spoon the filling inside. Pile on to a serving dish and pour a little chocolate fudge sauce over the top. Serve the remaining sauce separately.

Freezing: is recommended for the choux buns before filling. When cold, place in a rigid container and freeze. These will keep for up to 3 months. Defrost at room temperature for 1 hour and fill as above.

SERVES 4-6

Nutritional content per serving:	Carbohydrate: 16 g	Fat: 31 g	Fibre: 1 g	Kilocalories: 363

CHOCOLATE JELLY MOULD

FOR A DESSERT WITH A LESS FIRM MIXTURE, YOU CAN OMIT THE GELATINE AND SERVE THIS IN INDIVIDUAL DISHES

1 × 113 g (4 oz) carton skimmed milk, soft
    cheese or curd cheese
25 g (1 oz) caster sugar
6 tablespoons milk
75 g (3 oz) plain chocolate, melted
2 tablespoons water
2 teaspoons powdered gelatine
1 × 142 ml (5 fl oz) carton whipping cream,
    whipped
White Chocolate Caraque (see page 7) to
    decorate (optional)

Place the cheese in a bowl and beat until softened. Stir in the sugar and milk then add the chocolate and mix well.

Place the water in a small bowl and sprinkle the gelatine on top. Set aside for 2 minutes until spongy. Place the bowl in simmering water until the gelatine has melted. Stir thoroughly. Cool, then add to the chocolate mixture with the whipped cream. Mix well, then spoon into a dampened 600 ml (1 pint) jelly mould.

Leave the jelly in the refrigerator until set. Dip the mould briefly into hot water, then turn out on to a serving plate. Decorate with white chocolate caraque, if desired.

SERVES 4

Nutritional content per serving:	Carbohydrate: 24 g	Fat: 20 g	Fibre: 0.5 g	Kilocalories: 308

CHOCOLATE GINGER TRIFLE

6 trifle sponges
6 teaspoons ginger preserve extra jam
1 × 298 g (10½ oz) can mandarin oranges
    in natural juice
3 tablespoons orange-flavoured liqueur
2 pieces stem ginger, chopped
25 g (1 oz) caster sugar
25 g (1 oz) cornflour
1 tablespoon cocoa powder
600 ml (1 pint) milk
2 egg yolks
TO DECORATE:
1 × 142 ml (5 fl oz) carton whipping cream,
    whipped
stem ginger, sliced
Chocolate Curls (see page 7)

Split the trifle sponges in half and spread with the ginger preserve jam. Arrange on the base of a 1.2 litre (2 pint) trifle bowl. Drain the mandarins, reserving 4 tablespoons of the juice. Spoon the liqueur over the sponges with the reserved juice. Spoon the mandarins and ginger over the sponges.

Combine the sugar, cornflour, cocoa powder and milk in a saucepan and heat, whisking constantly until smooth and thickened. Continue to cook, stirring, for 2 minutes. Cool slightly, then beat in the egg yolks. Set aside, stirring frequently, until cold, then spoon the chocolate custard over the fruit.

Pipe whipped cream around the rim. Decorate with the stem ginger and chocolate curls.

Microwave: Combine the sugar, cornflour, cocoa powder and milk in a large jug and microwave on Full Power for 6 minutes, stirring once after 3 minutes.

SERVES 6

Nutritional content per serving: Carbohydrate: 39 g   Fat: 18 g   Fibre: 1 g   Kilocalories: 353

CHOCOLATE ORANGE ROULADE

4 eggs, separated
175 g (6 oz) caster sugar
40 g (1½ oz) cocoa powder
icing sugar, sifted
FILLING:
1 × 142 ml (5 fl oz) carton double cream
150 g (5 oz) natural fromage frais
2 tablespoons icing sugar, sifted
finely grated rind of 1 orange
1 tablespoon orange-flavoured liqueur

In a mixing bowl, whisk the egg yolks and sugar until thick and creamy. Sift the cocoa powder over the mixture and fold in thoroughly. In a second bowl, whisk the egg whites until stiff and gently fold into the chocolate mixture.

Spoon into a greased and lined 30 × 20 cm (12 × 8 inch) Swiss roll tin and level the surface. Bake in a preheated oven, 180°C, 350°F, Gas Mark 4 for 25-30 minutes or until firm. Cool for 5 minutes, then cover with a damp tea towel and leave to become completely cold.

Sift icing sugar over a large sheet of greaseproof paper. Invert the cake on to the paper and carefully peel off the lining paper.

Place the double cream in a bowl and whip until thick. Add the fromage frais, icing sugar, orange rind and liqueur. Mix gently. Spread the mixture over the cake, then roll up like a Swiss roll with the help of the greaseproof paper. Transfer the roulade to a serving dish, dust with more icing sugar if needed, and serve within 2 hours. The cake may crack when rolled; this is quite normal.

SERVES 6-8

Nutritional content per serving: Carbohydrate: 42 g   Fat: 17 g   Kilocalories: 351

DANISH CHOCOLATE PUDDING

3 dessert apples, peeled, cored and sliced

2 large dessert pears, peeled, cored and sliced

1 tablespoon water

25 g (1 oz) granulated sugar (optional)

50 g (2 oz) butter

150 g (5 oz) fresh wholemeal breadcrumbs

25 g (1 oz) brown sugar

25 g (1 oz) drinking chocolate

1 large chocolate flake to decorate

Place the apples, pears and water in a saucepan. Stir in the sugar, if using, and heat gently for 10 minutes or until the fruit is soft.

Melt the butter in a saucepan over a gentle heat. Stir in the breadcrumbs, brown sugar and drinking chocolate. Stir over a moderate heat for 10-15 minutes or until the mixture becomes toasted and has a crisp texture.

Layer the fruit and crumbs in a 600 ml (1 pint) dish, finishing with a layer of crumbs. Crumble the chocolate flake and sprinkle over the top. Serve cold, with Chocolate Sauce (see page 92), natural yogurt or single cream.

Microwave: Cook the apples and pears with the water in a bowl on Full Power for 4 minutes, stirring once.

SERVES 4

Nutritional content per serving: Carbohydrate: 55 g   Fat: 14 g   Fibre: 6 g   Kilocalories: 355

Chocolate Orange Roulade; Danish Chocolate Pudding; Chocolate Ginger Trifle

CHOCOLATE MERINGUE PIE

125 g (4 oz) plain flour
50 g (2 oz) margarine
15 g (½ oz) icing sugar, sifted
1 egg yolk
2 tablespoons water
FILLING AND TOPPING:
25 g (1 oz) cornflour
2 eggs, separated
300 ml (½ pint) milk
125 g (4 oz) plain chocolate, broken
125 g (4 oz) caster sugar

Sift the flour into a mixing bowl and rub in the margarine until the mixture resembles fine breadcrumbs. Stir in the icing sugar, then add the egg yolk and water and mix to a stiff dough. Turn on to a floured surface and knead until smooth. Wrap in foil and chill in the refrigerator for 30 minutes. Roll out the pastry to line an 18 cm (7 inch) flan tin or dish. Prick the pastry base, then bake blind in a preheated oven, 190°C, 375°F, Gas Mark 5 for 15 minutes. Remove the lining and return to the oven for 5 minutes more.

Mix together the cornflour and egg yolks. Heat the milk in a saucepan until almost boiling, then pour on to the egg mixture, stirring constantly. Return to the saucepan, add the chocolate and heat, stirring, until the chocolate melts and the sauce thickens. Continue to cook for 1 minute, cool slightly, and pour into the pastry case. Set aside to cool completely, covering with clingfilm.

Whisk the egg whites until stiff, then whisk in the sugar 1 tablespoon at a time. Pipe on to the chocolate mixture and bake in a preheated oven, 190°C, 375°F, Gas Mark 5 for 9-12 minutes or until golden. Serve either warm or cold, with cream or natural fromage frais.

SERVES 4-6

Nutritional content per serving: Carbohydrate: 91 g   Fat: 28 g   Fibre: 2 g   Kilocalories: 638

Chocolate Meringue Pie

Chocolate Fruit and Nut Flan

CHOCOLATE FRUIT AND NUT FLAN

175 g (6 oz) plain flour
pinch of salt
40 g (1½ oz) margarine
40 g (1½ oz) lard
1½ tablespoons water
FILLING:
2 eggs
50 g (2 oz) caster sugar
125 g (4 oz) mixed nuts, chopped
125 g (4 oz) mixed dried fruit
50 g (2 oz) mixed fresh breadcrumbs
1 tablespoon lemon juice
1 tablespoon rum
TOPPING:
125 g (4 oz) plain chocolate, melted

Sift the flour and salt into a mixing bowl. Rub in the margarine and lard until the mixture resembles fine breadcrumbs. Add the water and mix to a firm dough. Turn on to a lightly floured surface and knead until smooth. Roll out the pastry to line a 20-23 cm (8-9 inch) flan tin or dish, then prick the base.

Make the filling. Place the eggs and sugar in a bowl and whisk until pale and thick. Stir in the nuts, mixed dried fruit, breadcrumbs, lemon juice and rum, then mix well. Spoon into the pastry case, place the tin or dish on a baking sheet, and bake in a preheated oven, 190°C, 375°F, Gas Mark 5, for 25-35 minutes or until set and golden.

Allow the flan to cool, then spread the melted chocolate over the top. Leave to set. Serve with natural fromage frais.

Freezing: is recommended. Wrap with tin foil and seal in a freezer bag. It will keep for up to 4 months. Defrost at room temperature for 3 hours.

SERVES 6-8

Nutritional content per serving: Carbohydrate: 64 g   Fat: 30 g   Fibre: 5 g   Kilocalories: 555

ICE CREAMS

MOUTH-WATERING ICE CREAMS CAN BE MADE AND THEN STORED IN THE FREEZER READY FOR AN UNEXPECTED VISIT FROM FRIENDS OR A REFRESHING SURPRISE FOR THE FAMILY ON A HOT SUMMER DAY. FOR EXTRA CHOCOLATE FLAVOUR, SERVE THEM WITH A SAUCE (SEE PAGES 92 AND 95)

Frozen chocolate orange soufflé

4 eggs
125 g (4 oz) caster sugar
grated rind and juice of 1 orange
1 tablespoon drinking chocolate
50 g (2 oz) plain chocolate, melted
1 × 284ml (10 fl oz) carton double cream,
  whipped
TO DECORATE:
Chocolate Leaves (see page 8)
fine strands of orange rind

Tie a double band of foil or greaseproof paper very tightly around a 600 ml (1 pint) soufflé dish to stand 5 cm (2 inches) above the dish. Set the dish aside.

Place the egg yolks, sugar and orange rind in a bowl and whisk until pale and thick. In a cup, mix the drinking chocolate to a paste with the orange juice and stir into the melted chocolate. Whisk all of this into the egg mixture.

In a second bowl whisk the egg whites until stiff and fold into the mixture with the cream. Pour into the prepared dish and freeze until the ice cream is firm.

Carefully remove the paper and transfer the soufflé to the refrigerator 15 minutes before serving to soften it slightly. To serve, decorate the soufflé with chocolate leaves and orange rind.

SERVES 4-6

Nutritional content per serving: Carbohydrate: 50 g   Fat: 46 g   Fibre: 0.5 g   Kilocalories: 632

Chocolate mint ice cream

TRY SERVING A TRIO OF ICE CREAMS SUCH AS CHOCOLATE MINT, CHOCOLATE AND CHOCOLATE MAPLE IN CHOCOLATE CASES (SEE PAGES 8 AND 9). A CHOCOLATE SAUCE AND BISCUITS WOULD MAKE A SUITABLE ACCOMPANIMENT.

125 g (4 oz) white chocolate, broken
65 ml (2½ fl oz) single cream
1 × 284 ml (10 fl oz) carton double cream,
  whipped
40 g (1½ oz) icing sugar, sifted
½ teaspoon peppermint flavouring
25 g (1 oz) chocolate mint sticks, chopped
green food colouring
chocolate mint sticks to serve (optional)

Place the chocolate and single cream in a heatproof bowl and place over a saucepan of gently simmering water. Stir until the chocolate has melted.

In a large bowl blend a little of the whipped double cream with the chocolate mixture. Stir in the icing sugar, then combine with the remaining whipped cream. Stir in the peppermint flavouring, chocolate mint sticks and enough colouring to tint the mixture green. Mix thoroughly and spoon into a rigid container.

Freeze for 2 hours, then spoon into a bowl and beat until smooth. Return to the rinsed container and freeze again until firm.

Transfer the ice cream to the refrigerator 15 minutes before serving to soften it slightly. Spoon into individual dishes and serve at once, with chocolate mint sticks, if using.

Microwave: Melt the white chocolate and single cream in a bowl on Full Power for 1 minute.

SERVES 4-6

Nutritional content per serving: Carbohydrate: 36 g   Fat: 39 g   Kilocalories: 504

Frozen Chocolate Orange Soufflé; Chocolate Mint Ice Cream

CHOCOLATE MAPLE ICE CREAM

50 g (2 oz) raisins
4 tablespoons boiling water
2 egg yolks
50 g (2 oz) soft brown sugar
50 g (2 oz) plain chocolate, broken
3 tablespoons maple syrup
1 × 284 ml (10 fl oz) carton double cream,
   whipped

Place the raisins in a bowl and add the boiling water. Leave to soak for 15 minutes, then drain and set aside.

In a large bowl, whisk the egg yolks and sugar together until thick and pale. Combine the chocolate and maple syrup in a heatproof bowl and place over a saucepan of gently simmering water. Stir until the chocolate has melted. Allow to cool, then mix with the egg mixture and fold in the whipped cream. Mix well, then spoon into a rigid container, seal and freeze for 1-2 hours.

Spoon the ice cream into a bowl and beat until smooth, then fold in the raisins. Return to the rinsed container, seal and freeze until the ice cream is firm.

Transfer the ice cream to the refrigerator 15 minutes before serving to soften it slightly. Serve with langues de chat or Chocolate Viennese Biscuits (see page 76).

Microwave: Melt the chocolate with the maple syrup in a bowl on Full Power for 1½ minutes.

SERVES 4-6

Nutritional content per serving: Carbohydrate: 40 g   Fat: 42 g   Fibre: 1 g   Kilocalories: 543

MINI CHOCOLATE CASTLES

50 g (2 oz) plain chocolate, melted
1 tablespoon cocoa powder
1 tablespoon boiling water
1 tablespoon brandy
1 egg white
50 g (2 oz) caster sugar
1 × 142 ml (5 fl oz) carton whipping cream,
   lightly whipped
White Chocolate Curls (see page 7) to
   decorate

Chill 4 ramekins in the freezer for 5 minutes, then pour a quarter of the melted chocolate into each ramekin and rotate to cover the bases completely.

In a cup, mix the cocoa powder to a paste with the water. Stir in the brandy and set aside. Place the egg white in a bowl and whisk until stiff, then whisk in the sugar 1 tablespoon at a time.

In a large bowl, blend the whipped cream and the cooled cocoa and brandy mixture. Fold in the egg white and mix lightly but thoroughly. Divide the mixture between the 4 ramekins. Cover with foil and freeze until firm.

Dip the ramekins into hot water then invert on individual serving dishes. Decorate with white chocolate curls, and serve with a jug of single cream.

SERVES 4

Nutritional content per serving: Carbohydrate: 23 g   Fat: 13 g   Kilocalories: 220

Rhubarb and Chocolate Ice Cream; Mini Chocolate Castles; Chocolate Maple Ice Cream

RHUBARB AND CHOCOLATE ICE CREAM

500 g (1 lb) rhubarb, sliced
125 g (4 oz) caster sugar
2 tablespoons water .
2 egg whites
75 g (3 oz) icing sugar
1 × 142 ml (5 fl oz) carton double cream,
   whipped
75 g (3 oz) plain chocolate, chopped

Place the rhubarb, sugar and water in a saucepan and cook gently for 15 minutes or until the fruit is soft. Cool slightly, then purée in a blender or food processor. Transfer the fruit purée to a large bowl and set aside.

In a bowl, whisk the egg whites until stiff, then whisk in the icing sugar 1 tablespoon at a time. Fold into the rhubarb purée with the whipped double cream and chocolate. Spoon into a rigid container, seal and freeze until firm.

Transfer the ice cream to the refrigerator 15 minutes before serving to soften it slightly. Spoon into individual dishes to serve.

SERVES 6

Nutritional content per serving: Carbohydrate: 44 g   Fat: 16 g   Fibre: 2 g   Kilocalories: 316

BOMBE CHOCOLAT

1 × 284 ml (10 fl oz) carton double cream
65 ml (2½ fl oz) single cream
125 g (4 oz) plain chocolate, melted
1–2 tablespoons rum
125 g (4 oz) meringues (see Chocolate
  Meringue Torte, page 54), crumbled
Chocolate Fudge Sauce (see page 92) to
  serve

Combine the double and single cream in a bowl and whip. Blend a little of the whipped cream with the melted chocolate and then stir in the rum.

Add the meringues to the remaining whipped cream and mix well. Add the chocolate mixture, swirling it through to give a marbled effect. Spoon into a 1.2 litre (2 pint) pudding basin, cover with a lid or foil and freeze until firm.

Dip the basin in hot water then turn the bombe out on to a serving plate. Transfer to the refrigerator for 20-25 minutes before serving to soften the bombe slightly. Serve with the chocolate fudge sauce in a separate jug.

SERVES 6

Nutritional content per serving: Carbohydrate: 58 g   Fat: 41 g   Fibre: 1 g   Kilocalories: 623

Bombe Chocolat

Speckled Mango Ice Cream

SPECKLED MANGO ICE CREAM

2 mangoes
2 tablespoons lemon juice
2 egg whites
50 g (2 oz) caster sugar
1 × 142 ml (5 fl oz) carton whipping cream, whipped
1 large chocolate flake, crushed
25 g (1 oz) plain chocolate, chopped

Cut the mangoes in half, remove the stones and scoop out the flesh. Purée with the lemon juice in a blender or food processor, transfer to a large bowl and set aside.

In a second bowl, whisk the egg whites until stiff, then whisk in the sugar 1 tablespoon at a time. Fold into the mango purée with the whipped cream, chocolate flake and chocolate. Mix well, then spoon into a rigid container, seal and freeze until firm.

Transfer the ice cream to the refrigerator 15 minutes before serving to soften it slightly. Scoop into individual glass bowls and serve with a fruit salad or Quick Chocolate Sauce (see page 92).

SERVES 6

Nutritional content per serving: Carbohydrate: 33 g   Fat: 12 g   Fibre: 2 g   Kilocalories: 247

Apricot and chocolate iced loaf

1 × 411 g (14½ oz) can apricot halves in
  fruit juice
2 eggs, separated
125 g (4 oz) caster sugar
1 × 284 ml (10 fl oz) carton whipping
  cream, whipped
50 g (2 oz) skimmed milk soft cheese or
  curd cheese
65 ml (2½ fl oz) whipping cream
125 g (4 oz) plain chocolate, melted
TO DECORATE:
65 ml (2½ fl oz) whipping cream, whipped
Chocolate Triangles (see page 7)

Drain and discard most of the juice from the can of apricots, then place the fruit and remaining juice in a blender or food processor. Process to a purée and set aside.

Place the egg yolks in a bowl with half the caster sugar and whisk until pale and thick. In a second bowl, whisk the egg whites until stiff, then whisk in the remaining sugar 1 tablespoon at a time. Fold all this into the egg yolks and mix thoroughly. Carefully fold in the whipped cream and the prepared apricot purée. Spoon the mixture into a rigid container and freeze until just hard, about 4 hours.

Meanwhile, beat the cheese with the 65 ml (2½ fl oz) whipping cream in a bowl. Add the melted chocolate and mix well. Set aside.

Turn the apricot ice cream into a bowl and beat until smooth. Place one third of the mixture in a greased 1 kg (2 lb) loaf tin. Drop about half the chocolate mixture in spoonfuls over the ice cream. Top with half the remaining ice cream, then drop the remaining chocolate mixture in spoonfuls on top. Finish the loaf by spreading ice cream lightly over the surface. Cover with foil and freeze until firm.

About 15 minutes before serving, turn the loaf on to a serving plate and decorate with piped, whipped cream and chocolate triangles. Place in the refrigerator until required.

SERVES 8-10

Nutritional content per serving:	Carbohydrate: 40 g	Fat: 26 g	Fibre: 1 g	Kilocalories: 399

Chocolate ice cream

2 eggs, separated
65 ml (2½ fl oz) double cream
50 g (2 oz) caster sugar
1 × 170 g (6 oz) can evaporated milk,
  chilled
125 g (4 oz) plain chocolate, melted

In a bowl, combine the egg yolks and double cream, mix well and set aside. In a large bowl, whisk the egg whites until stiff, then whisk in the sugar, 1 tablespoon at a time. Whisk the yolks into the whites.

Place the chilled evaporated milk in a large jug or bowl and whisk until thick. Fold into the egg mixture. Blend a little of the mixture with the chocolate, then stir into the egg and evaporated milk mixture. Mix well and spoon into a rigid container. Freeze until firm.

Transfer the ice cream to the refrigerator 15 minutes before serving to soften it slightly. Serve on its own or with fresh fruit, a chocolate sauce or biscuits.

SERVES 4-6

Nutritional content per serving:	Carbohydrate: 39 g	Fat: 24 g	Fibre: 1 g	Kilocalories: 394

Chocolate Ice Cream; Mocha Ice Cream; Apricot and Chocolate Iced Loaf

MOCHA ICE CREAM

2 teaspoons instant coffee granules

150 ml (¼ pint) milk

50 g (2 oz) plain chocolate, melted in a
   large bowl

1 egg white

50 g (2 oz) caster sugar

75 ml (3 fl oz) whipping cream, whipped

25 g (1 oz) walnuts, chopped finely

walnuts, chopped, to decorate

Place the coffee granules and milk in a saucepan and heat until almost boiling. Gradually pour on to the melted chocolate, mixing well, then set the mocha mixture aside to cool.

In a bowl, whisk the egg white until stiff, then whisk in the sugar 1 tablespoon at a time. Fold into the mocha mixture with the whipped cream and walnuts. Pour into a rigid container, seal and freeze until firm. Remove from the freezer 5 minutes before serving and leave at room temperature to soften slightly before spooning into individual bowls and decorating with chopped walnuts.

SERVES 4

Nutritional content per serving: Carbohydrate: 24 g   Fat: 15 g   Fibre: 1 g   Kilocalories: 237

CHOCOLATE PEACHES

1 × 411 g (14½ oz) can peaches in fruit
  juice, drained
4 scoops Chocolate Ice Cream (see
  page 42)
½ quantity Chocolate Sauce (see page 92)
1 × 142 ml (5 fl oz) carton whipping cream,
  whipped
Chocolate Curls (see page 7) to decorate

Divide half the fruit between 4 tall sundae glasses. Add a scoop of ice cream to each, then top with the remaining fruit. Pour the sauce over, then pipe large whirls of whipped cream on top. Decorate with chocolate curls and serve at once.

SERVES 4

Nutritional content per serving: Carbohydrate: 45 g Fat: 31 g Fibre: 1 g Kilocalories: 485

TIPSY CHRISTMAS ICE CREAM

PACKED WITH DRIED FRUIT AND FLAVOURED WITH RUM AND SHERRY, THIS MAKES AN IDEAL ALTERNATIVE TO CHRISTMAS PUDDING

25 g (1 oz) raisins
25 g (1 oz) glacé cherries, chopped
50 g (2 oz) mixed dried fruit
3 tablespoons rum
3 tablespoons sherry
450 ml (¾ pint) single cream
3 egg yolks
75 g (3 oz) soft brown sugar
125 g (4 oz) plain chocolate, melted
finely grated rind of 1 orange
1 × 142 ml (5 fl oz) carton double cream,
   whipped

Combine the raisins, cherries and mixed dried fruit in a bowl. Add the rum and sherry, stir and leave to soak for 4 hours or overnight.

Heat the single cream gently to simmering point. Place the egg yolks in a large bowl with the sugar and whisk until thick and pale. Add the hot cream, stirring constantly, then strain the mixture back into the clean saucepan.

Heat gently, stirring until the mixture thickens and coats the back of a spoon. Cover the surface with clingfilm or damp greaseproof paper and leave to cool. Gently fold in the melted chocolate, orange rind and whipped double cream, then mix lightly but thoroughly. Transfer to a rigid container, seal and freeze for 1 hour. Spoon into a bowl and beat the mixture until smooth. Return to the rinsed container, seal and freeze again. Repeat after 1 hour, then fold in the fruit, transfer to a 900 ml (1½ pint) pudding basin, and cover with foil or clingfilm. Freeze until the ice cream is firm.

Transfer the ice cream to the refrigerator 15 minutes before serving to soften slightly. Dip the basin in hot water, then turn the bombe out on to a serving plate and serve immediately.

SERVES 6

Nutritional content per serving:	Carbohydrate: 40 g	Fat: 38 g	Fibre: 1 g	Kilocalories: 536

EDWARDIAN RUM ICE CREAM

50 g (2 oz) wholemeal breadcrumbs
25 g (1 oz) walnuts, chopped finely
50 g (2 oz) soft brown sugar
1 egg, separated
1 × 150 g (5.2 oz) carton natural yogurt
40 g (1½ oz) plain chocolate, grated
1 tablespoon rum or 1 teaspoon rum
   flavouring

In a small bowl, combine the breadcrumbs, walnuts and half of the sugar. Mix well. Spread the mixture over a baking sheet lined with foil, then place under a preheated grill for 2 minutes or until the mixture is toasted and golden. Allow to cool.

Beat the egg white in a mixing bowl until stiff, then whisk in the remaining sugar. In another bowl, mix the egg yolk with the yogurt, then stir in the toasted crumb mixture and grated chocolate. Fold in the egg white with the rum and spoon into a rigid container. Freeze until firm.

Transfer the ice cream to the refrigerator for 15 minutes before serving to soften it slightly. Spoon into bowls and serve with a jug of Quick Chocolate Sauce (see page 92).

SERVES 4

Nutritional content per serving:	Carbohydrate: 27 g	Fat: 8 g	Fibre: 2 g	Kilocalories: 210

Chocolate Peaches; Edwardian Rum Ice Cream; Tipsy Christmas Ice Cream

GÂTEAUX AND CHEESECAKES

A CHOCOLATE RECIPE BOOK WOULD NOT BE COMPLETE WITHOUT IMPRESSIVE-
LOOKING GÂTEAUX AND CHEESECAKES. THE EXTRA TIME AND ENERGY REQUIRED TO
MAKE THEM WILL BE REWARDED WITH RESULTS THAT ARE BOTH A DELIGHT TO THE
EYE AND THE PALATE.

BLACK FOREST GÂTEAU

3 eggs
75 g (3 oz) caster sugar
75 g (3 oz) plain flour
1½ tablespoons cocoa powder
1½ teaspoons baking powder
2 tablespoons hot water
FILLING AND DECORATION:
1 × 142 ml (5 fl oz) carton double cream
65 ml (2½ fl oz) single cream
1½ tablespoons Kirsch
1 × 400 g (14 oz) can cherry pie filling
25 g (1 oz) plain chocolate, grated

In a bowl, whisk the eggs with the sugar until the mixture is pale and thick and the whisk leaves a trail. Sift together the flour, cocoa and baking powder, then fold into the egg mixture with the water.

Grease and line the base of 2 × 18 cm (7 inch) sandwich tins and divide the cake mixture between them. Bake in a preheated oven, 190°C, 375°F, Gas Mark 5 for 20 minutes or until well risen and firm. Invert the cakes on to a wire rack to cool.

Combine the double and single creams in a bowl and whisk until stiff. Place 1 cake layer on a board and spoon over half the Kirsch. Spoon one third of the cream into a piping bag and pipe a ring around the edge of the cake. Reserve the remaining cream.

Reserve 6 cherries for decoration. Remove most of the sauce from the remaining cherries. Spoon the fruit inside the band of cream. Spoon the rest of the Kirsch over the other cake layer and place on top of the cherries. Spread the cake top and sides with some of the reserved cream and sprinkle with grated chocolate. Pipe on the remaining cream and decorated with cherries.

SERVES 6-8

Nutritional content per serving: Carbohydrate: 45 g   Fat: 19 g   Fibre: 2 g   Kilocalories: 373

MOCHA CHEESECAKE

50 g (2 oz) butter, melted
125 g (4 oz) bourbon biscuits, crushed
FILLING:
1 × 227 g (8 oz) carton skimmed milk soft
   cheese or curd cheese
2 eggs, separated
50 g (2 oz) caster sugar
1 × 142 ml (5 fl oz) carton single cream
2 teaspoons instant coffee granules
4 tablespoons hot water
15 g (½ oz) powdered gelatine
75 g (3 oz) plain chocolate, melted
TOPPING:
whole hazelnuts
25 g (1 oz) plain chocolate, melted
65 ml (2½ fl oz) double cream, whipped

Mix the melted butter with the biscuit crumbs in a bowl. Press on to the base of a greased 20 cm (8 inch) loose-bottomed or springform cake tin. Leave in a cool place to set.

Meanwhile place the cheese in a large bowl, beat to soften slightly, then beat in the egg yolks, sugar and single cream. Dissolve the coffee granules in the hot water in a small bowl and leave to cool.

Sprinkle the gelatine over the surface of the cold coffee. Set aside for 2 minutes until spongy. Place the bowl in a saucepan of simmering water until the gelatine has melted. Stir thoroughly. When cool, but still liquid, add to the cheese mixture with the chocolate. Mix well.

Whisk the egg whites until stiff and fold into the mixture. Pour over the biscuit base and chill in the refrigerator. When set, transfer to a serving plate and return to the refrigerator.

Dip the hazelnuts into the chocolate and leave to set on greaseproof paper. Decorate with cream and the hazelnuts.

SERVES 6-8

Nutritional content per serving: Carbohydrate: 36 g   Fat: 32 g   Fibre: 1 g   Kilocalories: 472

Black Forest Gâteau; Mocha Cheesecake

CHOCOLATE BLACKCURRANT RING

30 g (1¼ oz) butter, melted
4 eggs
125 g (4 oz) caster sugar
75 g (3 oz) plain flour
25 g (1 oz) cocoa powder
FILLING:
250 g (8 oz) blackcurrants
50 g (2 oz) granulated or caster sugar
1 tablespoon water
1 × 142 ml (5 fl oz) carton double cream,
  whipped
2 tablespoons blackcurrant yogurt

Brush a 1.2 litre (2 pint) ring mould with a little of the melted butter.

In a large bowl, whisk the eggs and sugar together until pale and thick. Sift the flour and cocoa powder together and fold half into the egg mixture. Stir in the remaining melted butter, then fold in the remaining flour mixture. Pour into the prepared ring mould and bake in a preheated oven, 180°C, 350°F, Gas Mark 4 for 15-20 minutes or until well risen and firm to touch.

Turn the cake ring out on a wire rack to cool. Combine the blackcurrants, sugar and water in a saucepan and heat gently until the fruit is soft and cooked. Allow to cool. Spoon a little of the whipped cream into a piping bag fitted with a star nozzle and set aside. Mix the remaining cream with the blackcurrants and yogurt.

Cut the cake in half horizontally and sandwich together with the blackcurrant cream. Decorate with the reserved whipped cream.

Freezing: is recommended before decorating. When cold wrap with tin foil and seal in a freezer bag. This will keep for up to 3 months. Defrost in the refrigerator for 5-6 hours and decorate as above.

SERVES 6

Nutritional content per serving:	Carbohydrate: 48 g	Fat: 22 g	Fibre: 4 g	Kilocalories: 411

CHOCOLATE CHEESECAKE FLAN

125 g (4 oz) shortcrust pastry (see
  Chocolate-Coated Tarts, page 64)
FILLING:
250 g (8 oz) full-fat cream cheese
2 eggs, separated
25 g (1 oz) caster sugar
75 g (3 oz) plain chocolate, melted
1 tablespoon sherry
TO DECORATE:
65 ml (2½ fl oz) double cream, whipped
White Chocolate Caraque (see page 7)

Roll out the pastry to line a 20 cm (8 inch) fluted flan tin or dish. Prick the base and bake blind (lined with greaseproof paper and baking beans) in a preheated oven, 190°C, 375°F, Gas Mark 5 for 12 minutes. Remove the lining and cook for 5 minutes.

Make the filling. Place the cream cheese in a bowl and beat in the egg yolks, sugar, melted chocolate and sherry. In a second bowl, whisk the egg whites until stiff and fold into the chocolate mixture. Spoon into the flan case and return to the oven for 25-30 minutes or until the filling is set. Allow to cool, then chill until required.

Decorate with whipped cream and white chocolate caraque.

Freezing: is recommended before decorating. Freeze without wrapping until hard. Wrap with tin foil and seal in a freezer bag. This will keep for up to 3 months. Defrost in the refrigerator for 5-6 hours.

SERVES 6-8

Nutritional content per serving:	Carbohydrate: 28 g	Fat: 38 g	Fibre: 1 g	Kilocalories: 470

LEMON DELIGHT

3 eggs
75 g (3 oz) caster sugar
75 g (3 oz) plain flour
finely grated rind of ½ lemon
2 tablespoons lemon juice
2 tablespoons sherry
FILLING:
½ quantity Chocolate Fudge Frosting (see
  page 91)
TOPPING:
1 × 113 g (4 oz) carton skimmed milk soft
  cheese or curd cheese
grated rind of ½ lemon
2–3 tablespoons single cream
15 g (½ oz) icing sugar, sifted
Chocolate Leaves (see page 8) to decorate

In a large bowl, whisk the eggs with the sugar until the mixture is pale and thick and the whisk leaves a trail. Sift the flour and fold into the mixture with the lemon rind. Grease 2 × 18 cm (7 inch) sandwich tins, line the bases, and spoon in the cake mixture.

Bake in a preheated oven, 190°C, 375°F, Gas Mark 5 for 15-20 minutes or until the cake layers are firm and springy. Invert them on a wire rack to cool, then prick them all over with a fork. Mix together the lemon juice and sherry, then spoon over the cake layers.

Sandwich the cake layers together with the chocolate fudge frosting and place on a serving plate. In a bowl, beat the cheese until softened. Add the lemon rind, single cream and icing sugar and mix well. Spread the mixture over the top of the cake and decorate with chocolate leaves.

SERVES 6-8

Nutritional content per serving: Carbohydrate: 50 g   Fat: 10 g   Fibre: 1 g   Kilocalories: 318

Chocolate Blackcurrant Ring; Chocolate Cheesecake Flan; Lemon Delight

SPICED CHOCOLATE CHEESECAKE

125 g (4 oz) chocolate digestive biscuits, crushed
1 teaspoon mixed spice
50 g (2 oz) butter, melted
FILLING:
2 eggs
50 g (2 oz) caster sugar
1 × 227 g (8 oz) carton skimmed milk soft cheese or curd cheese
25 g (1 oz) ground almonds
½ teaspoon grated nutmeg
75 g (3 oz) plain chocolate, melted
65 ml (2½ fl oz) double cream
TO DECORATE:
65 ml (2½ fl oz) double cream, whipped
Chocolate Caraque (see page 7)

In a bowl, mix together the biscuit crumbs, mixed spice and melted butter. Press on to the base of a 20 cm (8 inch) loose-bottomed or springform cake tin.

Make the filling. Place the eggs and sugar in a jug or bowl and whisk until thick and creamy. In a separate bowl, beat the cheese until softened. Add the ground almonds, nutmeg, melted chocolate and cream and mix well. Gradually add the whisked egg mixture and mix.

Spoon over the biscuit base and bake in a preheated oven, 180°C, 350°F, Gas Mark 4 for 40-50 minutes or until firm. Cool in the tin, then transfer to a serving plate and chill in the refrigerator.

Just before serving, decorate the cheesecake with whipped cream and chocolate caraque.

Freezing: is recommended before decorating. Freeze the cheesecake, without wrapping, until hard then wrap with tin foil and seal in a freezer bag. This will keep for up to 3 months. Defrost in the refrigerator for 5-6 hours.

SERVES 6-8

Nutritional content per serving: Carbohydrate: 35 g   Fat: 28 g   Fibre: 2 g   Kilocalories: 429

Spiced Chocolate Cheesecake; Chocolate Meringue Gâteau; Chocolate Walnut Gâteau

CHOCOLATE MERINGUE GÂTEAU

4 egg whites
250 g (8 oz) caster sugar
FILLING:
½ × 439 g (15½ oz) can unsweetened
    chestnut purée
75 g (3 oz) plain chocolate, melted
1 tablespoon brandy
50 g (2 oz) icing sugar, sifted
1 × 284 ml (10 fl oz) carton whipping
    cream, whipped
25 g (1 oz) melted chocolate to decorate

In a large bowl, whisk the egg whites until stiff, then whisk in the sugar 1 tablespoon at a time. Place baking parchment on 2 baking sheets and mark a 23 cm (9 inch) circle on each. Pipe or spoon the meringue mixture into the circles. Baked in a preheated oven, 120°C, 250°F, Gas Mark ½ for 2 hours. Turn off the oven, leaving the meringues inside to cool gradually for about 8 hours or overnight.

Make the filling. Place the chestnut purée in a large bowl. Add the chocolate, brandy and icing sugar and mix well. Fold in half the cream, reserving the remainder in a piping bag. Use the chestnut cream to sandwich the meringue layers together.

Place the meringue gâteau on a serving plate. Decorate the top by piping the remaining cream in rosettes around the rim, then drizzle melted chocolate over the centre.

SERVES 8

Nutritional content per serving: Carbohydrate: 58 g   Fat: 18 g   Fibre: 2 g   Kilocalories: 402

CHOCOLATE WALNUT GÂTEAU

3 eggs
75 g (3 oz) caster sugar
50 g (2 oz) plain flour
25 g (1 oz) cocoa powder
FILLING AND TOPPING:
1 × 142 ml (5 fl oz) carton whipping cream,
    whipped
50 g (2 oz) walnuts, chopped finely
½ quantity Chocolate Buttercream Icing
    (see page 91)
1 teaspoon instant coffee granules
TO DECORATE:
3 large chocolate flakes
walnut halves

In a large bowl, whisk the eggs with the sugar until the mixture is pale and thick and the whisk leaves a trail. Sift the flour and cocoa powder together and fold into the egg mixture. Grease a 30 × 20 cm (12 × 8 inch) Swiss roll tin, line the base and pour in the mixture.

Bake in a preheated oven, 200°C, 400°F, Gas Mark 6 for 10-12 minutes or until firm. Carefully invert the cake on a wire rack to cool. Peel off the paper and cut the cake widthways into 3 equal pieces.

Make the filling. Mix the whipped cream with the walnuts and use to sandwich the 3 cake layers together. Prepare the chocolate buttercream icing (see page 91), mixing the coffee granules with the cocoa powder and boiling water listed in the buttercream recipe first. Spread the buttercream over the gâteau top and sides.

Cut each chocolate flake into 3 equal lengths, then shave into smaller pieces and press to the sides of the gâteau. Use the crumbled pieces that remain and walnut halves to decorate the top.

Freezing: is recommended. Freeze the gâteau without wrapping until hard, then wrap with tin foil, seal in a freezer bag and freeze again. This will keep for up to 3 months. Defrost in the refrigerator for about 5-6 hours.

SERVES 8-10

Nutritional content per serving: Carbohydrate: 40 g   Fat: 23 g   Fibre: 1 g   Kilocalories: 388

RASPBERRY CHOCOLATE PAVLOVA

3 egg whites
175 g (6 oz) caster sugar
2 tablespoons cocoa powder
TOPPING:
1 × 142 ml (5 fl oz) carton double cream
150 g (5 oz) Greek yogurt
1 tablespoon icing sugar, sifted
375 g (12 oz) fresh or frozen (just
  defrosted) raspberries
Chocolate Curls (see page 7) to decorate

Whisk the egg whites until stiff. Whisk in the sugar 1 tablespoon at a time. Sift the cocoa powder twice then fold into the egg whites carefully to avoid streaks. Place baking parchment on a baking sheet and mark a 20 cm (8 inch) circle. Spoon the meringue mixture into the circle, swirling it to an even thickness. With the back of a spoon, make a hollow in the centre, then place in a preheated oven, 140°C, 275°F, Gas Mark 1 for 1½ hours. Turn off the oven, leaving the meringue inside to cool gradually for 8 hours or overnight.

Peel off the baking parchment and transfer the meringue to a serving plate. Whip the cream in a bowl until thick, then stir in the yogurt, icing sugar and half the raspberries. About 30 minutes before serving, spoon the fruit cream into the centre of the meringue shell. Decorate with the remaining raspberries and chocolate curls.

SERVES 6-8

Nutritional content per serving: Carbohydrate: 41 g   Fat: 18 g   Fibre: 5 g   Kilocalories: 337

CHOCOLATE KIWI CHOUX

65 g (2½ oz) plain flour
150 ml (¼ pint) cold water
50 g (2 oz) butter or margarine
2 eggs, beaten
FILLING:
1 × 142 ml (5 fl oz) carton double cream
125 g (4 oz) plain chocolate, melted
3 kiwi fruit, sliced
TOPPING:
25 g (1 oz) plain chocolate, melted
icing sugar, sifted

Make the choux pastry. Sift the flour on to a sheet of greaseproof paper. Place the water and butter or margarine in a saucepan and bring to the boil. When the liquid rises in the pan, remove from the heat and immediately shoot in all the flour. Beat well until the mixture forms a smooth ball, leaving the sides of the pan clean.

Set the pan aside to cool slightly, then add the beaten eggs a little at a time, beating well. Grease a baking sheet and mark a 20 cm (8 inch) circle on it. Pipe the choux pastry around the edge of the circle. Bake in a preheated oven, 200°C, 400°F, Gas Mark 6 for 20 minutes. Make 2 slits in the sides of the choux cake to release the steam, then lower the temperature to 180°C, 350°F, Gas Mark 4 and return to the oven for 10 minutes more. Cool on a wire rack.

Make the filling. Place the double cream in a bowl and whip until thick, then fold in the melted chocolate and mix thoroughly.

Just before serving cut the choux cake in half horizontally. Spread the chocolate cream over the base, then arrange the slices of kiwi fruit on top. Top with the remaining choux layer. Drizzle melted chocolate over the top and dust with icing sugar. Serve immediately.

SERVES 4-6

Nutritional content per serving: Carbohydrate: 45 g   Fat: 42 g   Fibre: 2 g   Kilocalories: 579

Raspberry Chocolate Pavlova; Chocolate Kiwi Choux

MOCHA STRAWBERRY SLICE

8 sponge fingers
6 tablespoons cold strong black coffee
250 g (8 oz) strawberries, sliced
1 × 142 ml (5 fl oz) carton double cream
1 × 113 g (4 oz) carton skimmed milk soft
  cheese or curd cheese
40 g (1½ oz) soft brown sugar
125 g (4 oz) plain chocolate, melted
125 g (4 oz) digestive biscuits, crushed
2 tablespoons sherry
142 ml (5 fl oz) carton double cream
2 teaspoons cold strong black coffee

Line a 500 g (1 lb) loaf tin with clingfilm so that it extends 2.5 cm (1 inch) above the top. Arrange the sponge fingers sugar-side down on the base of the tin and pour over 5 tablespoons of the coffee. Arrange half the strawberries over the top. Combine the remaining tablespoon of coffee with the double cream in a bowl and whip until thick. Spread half of the cream over the strawberries.

In a second bowl, beat the cheese with the sugar until softened, then stir in the melted chocolate, biscuits and sherry. Mix well then quickly spread half the mixture over the cream. Set aside 12 of the remaining strawberry slices for decoration and arrange the rest in the tin, on top of the chocolate mixture. Spread the remaining coffee cream over the strawberries and top with the remaining chocolate mixture.

Chill the loaf in the refrigerator until set, then turn out, carefully removing the clingfilm. Whip the double cream and coffee until thick. Spread a thin layer over the top and sides. Pipe the rest on top and decorate with the reserved strawberry slices. Serve immediately.

SERVES 6-8

Nutritional content per serving: Carbohydrate: 45 g   Fat: 34 g   Fibre: 3 g   Kilocalories: 514

CHOCOLATE MINT CHEESECAKE

50 g (2 oz) margarine, melted
125 g (4 oz) digestive biscuits, crushed
40 g (1½ oz) plain chocolate, melted
FILLING:
375 g (12 oz) skimmed milk soft cheese or
  curd cheese
50 g (2 oz) caster sugar
200 ml (7 fl oz) single cream
½ teaspoon peppermint flavouring
3 tablespoons water
15 g (½ oz) powdered gelatine
50 g (2 oz) chocolate mint sticks, chopped
65 ml (2½ fl oz) whipping cream, whipped
TO DECORATE:
whipped cream
mint sprigs

Mix the margarine, biscuit crumbs and chocolate. Press on to the base of a 20 cm (8 inch) loose-bottomed cake tin. Leave in a cool place to set. Place the cheese and sugar in a bowl. Beat to soften slightly, then stir in the single cream and peppermint.

Place the water in a small bowl and sprinkle the gelatine on top. Set aside for 2 minutes until spongy. Place the bowl in a saucepan of simmering water, stirring occasionally, until the gelatine has melted. Allow to cool slightly, then fold into the cheese mixture with the chocolate mint sticks and whipped cream. Mix thoroughly, then spoon over the biscuit base. Chill until set. Transfer to a serving plate. Decorate with whipped cream and mint sprigs.

Freezing: is recommended before decorating. Freeze the cheesecake without wrapping, until hard, then wrap with tin foil and seal in a freezer bag. This will keep for up to 3 months. Defrost in the refrigerator for 5-6 hours and decorate as above.

SERVES 8

Nutritional content per serving: Carbohydrate: 29 g   Fat: 22 g   Fibre: 1 g   Kilocalories: 350

Mocha Strawberry Slice; Chocolate Mint Cheesecake; Chocolate Meringue Torte

CHOCOLATE MERINGUE TORTE

36 sponge fingers
grated rind and juice of 2 oranges
150 ml (¼ pint) orange juice
75 g (3 oz) sunflower margarine
75 g (3 oz) caster sugar
15 g (½ oz) cocoa powder
I egg yolk
25 g (I oz) walnuts, chopped
50 g (2 oz) plain chocolate, melted
I tablespoon sherry
I × 142 ml (5 fl oz) carton whipping cream,
  whipped
MERINGUES:
I egg white
50 g (2 oz) caster sugar

Crumble the sponge fingers into a bowl and add the orange rind and juice. Mix well and set aside until all the juice has been absorbed.

In a bowl, cream the margarine with the sugar until pale and fluffy. Stir in the cocoa powder, egg yolk, walnuts, melted chocolate and sherry. Mix thoroughly. Press half the sponge finger mixture into an 18 cm (7 inch) springform cake tin lined with foil. Spread the chocolate mixture over the top, then add the remaining sponge finger mixture. Cover and refrigerate until set.

Make the meringues. In a large bowl, whisk the egg white until stiff, then whisk in the sugar I tablespoon at a time. Using a piping bag fitted with a large star nozzle, pipe 8-10 small rosettes on a baking sheet lined with baking parchment. Bake in a preheated oven, 120°C, 250°F, Gas Mark ½ for I hour. Turn off the oven, leaving the meringues inside to cool gradually for several hours.

Turn out the torte and remove the foil. Cover with whipped cream, then arrange the meringues on top. Serve within I hour.

SERVES 8-10

Nutritional content per serving: Carbohydrate: 58 g   Fat: 22 g   Fibre: I g   Kilocalories: 445

Coconut Chocolate Cheesecake; Chocolate Apricot Cheesecake; Cranberry Gâteau

CHOCOLATE APRICOT CHEESECAKE

THIS CHEESECAKE WORKS EQUALLY WELL WITH FRESH OR CANNED PEACHES, PEARS, PLUMS OR MANDARIN ORANGES

50 g (2 oz) butter, melted
125 g (4 oz) digestive biscuits, crushed
FILLING:
1 × 411 g (14½ oz) can apricots in fruit
  juice, drained
1 × 227 g (8 oz) carton skimmed milk soft
  cheese or curd cheese
50 g (2 oz) caster sugar
150 g (5 oz) Greek yogurt
2 eggs, separated
125 g (4 oz) plain chocolate, melted
TOPPING:
1 × 142 ml (5 fl oz) carton soured cream
Chocolate Curls (see page 7)

Mix the melted butter with the biscuit crumbs in a bowl. Press on to the base of a greased, loose-bottomed 20 cm (8 inch) cake tin. Leave in a cool place to set.

Spoon the apricots over the base. In a large bowl, beat the cheese with the sugar until softened, then stir in the yogurt and egg yolks. Mix well, then stir in the melted chocolate.

Whisk the egg whites until stiff and fold into the mixture. Spoon over the apricots and bake in a preheated oven, 180°C, 350°F, Gas Mark 4 for 45 minutes-1 hour or until set.

Place the soured cream in a bowl and beat until smooth. Spread over the cheesecake. Lower the oven temperature to 150°C, 300°F, Gas Mark 2 and return the cheesecake to the oven for 15 minutes. Cool in the tin, then remove and transfer to a serving plate. Chill until required. To serve, decorate with chocolate curls.

SERVES 6-8

Nutritional content per serving: Carbohydrate: 52 g   Fat: 28 g   Fibre: 2 g   Kilocalories: 501

CRANBERRY GÂTEAU

4 eggs, separated
150 g (5 oz) icing sugar, sifted
65 g (2½ oz) plain flour
15 g (½ oz) cornflour
25 g (1 oz) cocoa powder
½ teaspoon baking powder
3 drops vanilla flavouring
1 tablespoon milk
FILLING:
½ × 185 g (6½ oz) jar cranberry sauce
1 × 142 ml (5 fl oz) carton double cream,
  whipped
TOPPING:
1 × 142 ml (5 fl oz) carton soured cream
150 g (5 oz) white chocolate, melted
2 tablespoons skimmed milk soft cheese or
  curd cheese, softened
Chocolate Leaves (see page 8)
Chocolate Caraque (see page 7)

To make the cake, combine the egg yolks and icing sugar in a large mixing bowl and whisk until pale and fluffy. In a separate bowl, whisk the egg whites until stiff and fold into the egg yolk mixture.

Sift together the plain flour, cornflour, cocoa powder and baking powder. Fold into the mixture with the vanilla flavouring and milk. Grease and line the bases of 3 × 18 cm (7 inch) sandwich tins and divide the mixture between them. Bake in a preheated oven, 180°C, 350°F, Gas Mark 4 for 12-15 minutes. Cool the cakes in the tins for 5 minutes, then invert on wire racks to cool completely.

Make the filling. Gently stir the cranberry sauce into the whipped double cream and use to sandwich the 3 cake layers together.

Stir the soured cream·for the topping into the melted white chocolate. Gradually add the cheese. Spread the mixture over the top and sides of the cake. Transfer to a serving plate, decorate with chocolate leaves and chocolate caraque and store in the refrigerator until required.

SERVES 8

Nutritional content per serving: Carbohydrate: 52 g   Fat: 23 g   Fibre: 1 g   Kilocalories: 436

COCONUT CHOCOLATE CHEESECAKE

50 g (2 oz) butter
50 g (2 oz) caster sugar
40 g (1½ oz) plain flour
75 g (3 oz) desiccated coconut
FILLING:
2 eggs, separated
50 g (2 oz) soft brown sugar
2 tablespoons cornflour
3 teaspoons cocoa powder
200 ml (7 fl oz) milk
1 × 227 g (8 oz) carton skimmed milk soft
  cheese or curd cheese
1 × 142 ml (5 fl oz) carton double cream,
  whipped
TOPPING:
grated chocolate
desiccated coconut

In a mixing bowl, cream the butter with the sugar until light and fluffy, then mix in the flour and coconut. Press the mixture on to the base and sides of a greased 23 cm (9 inch) flan dish. Chill for 30 minutes, then bake in a preheated oven, 180°C, 350°F, Gas Mark 4 for 15–20 minutes or until golden brown. Allow to cool.

Place the egg yolks in a large bowl. Add the brown sugar, cornflour and cocoa powder and mix well. Heat the milk in a saucepan until just boiling, then stir into the egg mixture. Return to the saucepan and cook, stirring until the mixture thickens. Cover the surface of the custard with dampened greaseproof and allow to cool.

Beat the cheese in a large bowl with a little of the cooled custard mixture then add the remaining custard. Mix well, then fold in half the whipped double cream, reserving the remainder for decoration.

In a separate bowl, whisk the egg whites until stiff. Fold into the cheese mixture, then spoon on to the coconut base in the flan dish. Chill until required. Just before serving, decorate with the reserved whipped cream, grated chocolate and coconut.

SERVES 6-8

Nutritional content per serving: Carbohydrate: 34 g   Fat: 33 g   Fibre: 4 g   Kilocalories: 470

FAMILY CAKES

IDEAL FOR FAMILY TREATS, CELEBRATIONS AND PICNICS, THERE ARE CAKES IN THIS CHAPTER TO SUIT EVERY OCCASION AND EVERY TASTE. HUNGRY KIDS ADORE THE CHOCOLATE-COATED TARTS AND GRANNY'S ICED CHOCOLATE SPONGE, WHILE THE MORE DISCERNING PALATE MIGHT APPRECIATE CHOCOLATE CARROT AND RAISIN CAKE.

CHOCOLATE CHESTNUT ECLAIRS

I quantity Choux Pastry (see Chocolate Ginger Profiteroles, page 31)
½ × 439 g (15½ oz) can unsweetened chestnut purée
150 g (5 oz) natural fromage frais
50 g (2 oz) icing sugar, sifted
50 g (2 oz) plain chocolate, melted

Place the choux pastry in a piping bag fitted with a 2 cm (¾ inch) plain nozzle. Pipe 8 × 8 cm (3½ inch) fingers, at least 7 cm (3 inches) apart on a greased baking sheet. Bake in a preheated oven, 200°C, 400°F, Gas Mark 6 for 15 minutes, then lower the temperature to 180°C, 350°F, Gas Mark 4 and bake for 10 minutes more.

Place the eclairs on a wire rack, slitting the sides to allow steam to escape. Leave to cool.

In a bowl, combine the chestnut purée, fromage frais and icing sugar. Mix well. Just before serving, split the eclairs and fill with the chestnut mixture. Spread the tops with melted chocolate.

Freezing: is recommended before filling and decorating. When cold, place the eclairs in a rigid container. They will keep for up to 2 months. Defrost at room temperature for 1 hour and fill and decorate as above.

MAKES 8

Nutritional content per serving: Carbohydrate: 27 g   Fat: 9 g   Fibre: 2 g   Kilocalories: 211

MOCHA SWISS ROLL

3 teaspoons instant coffee granules
1 tablespoon hot water
3 eggs
75 g (3 oz) caster sugar
65 g (2½ oz) plain flour
15 g (½ oz) cocoa powder
caster sugar to dredge
½ quantity Chocolate Buttercream Icing (see page 91)

Mix the coffee granules with the hot water in a cup until dissolved, then leave to cool.

Place the eggs and sugar in a bowl and whisk with an electric mixer or vigorously by hand until the mixture is pale and thick and the whisk leaves a trail. Sift the flour and cocoa powder into the mixture and fold in lightly with the coffee liquid. Pour into a greased and lined 30 × 20 cm (12 × 8 inch) Swiss roll tin and tilt until evenly distributed and level. Bake in a preheated oven, 200°C, 400°F, Gas Mark 6 for 10-12 minutes.

Meanwhile place a piece of greaseproof paper on a dampened tea towel and sprinkle with caster sugar (see step-by-step instructions, page 9). Invert the Swiss roll on to the paper and peel away the lining paper. Trim the edges and roll up with the help of the damp tea towel. Carefully transfer the roll on to a wire rack to cool.

Gently unroll the cake and spread with chocolate buttercream. Roll up again and sprinkle with extra caster sugar if wished.

MAKES 8-10 SLICES

Nutritional content per serving: Carbohydrate: 35 g   Fat: 9 g   Kilocalories: 233

Chocolate Chestnut Eclairs; Mocha Swiss Roll

CHOCOLATE CHIP SCONES

THESE CHOCOLATE-FLAVOURED SCONES TASTE BEST WHEN STILL WARM, SPLIT, BUTTERED AND COVERED WITH JAM

250 g (8 oz) self-raising flour
1 teaspoon baking powder
50 g (2 oz) margarine
6 tablespoons milk
2 tablespoons chocolate yogurt
50 g (2 oz) plain chocolate drops
milk for brushing

Sift the flour and baking powder into a bowl and rub in the margarine until the mixture resembles fine breadcrumbs. Add the milk, yogurt and chocolate drops, then mix to a stiff dough.

Turn the dough on to a floured surface and knead lightly until smooth. Roll out to a circle 2 cm (¾ inch) thick then, using a 6 cm (2½ inch) fluted cutter, make 8-10 scones. Place on a greased baking sheet, allowing space for expansion, then brush with milk. Bake the scones in a preheated oven, 220°C, 425°F, Gas Mark 7 for 12-15 minutes or until well risen and browned.

Transfer the scones to a wire rack to cool slightly. Serve warm.

Microwave: If the scones have become cold reheat on Defrost for 2 minutes.

MAKES 8-10

Nutritional content per serving: Carbohydrate: 30 g   Fat: 8 g   Fibre: 1 g   Kilocalories: 197

CHEQUERED CHOCOLATE CAKE

THIS ATTRACTIVE CAKE BECOMES MORE MOIST IF KEPT IN AN AIRTIGHT TIN FOR 1–3 DAYS AFTER DECORATING BUT BEFORE CUTTING

125 g (4 oz) plain flour
125 g (4 oz) wholemeal flour
25 g (1 oz) cocoa powder
150 g (5 oz) caster sugar
1½ teaspoons bicarbonate of soda
1½ teaspoons baking powder
pinch of salt
125 g (4 oz) sunflower margarine
200 ml (7 fl oz) milk
3 eggs
1½ tablespoons black treacle
TO DECORATE:
¾ quantity Vanilla Buttercream Icing
  (see page 91)
¾ quantity Chocolate Buttercream Icing
  (see page 91)
Chocolate Triangles (see page 7)

Sift the dry ingredients into a mixing bowl and mix well. Make a well in the centre and add the remaining ingredients. Beat well for 2-3 minutes. Grease and line the base of a 23 cm (9 inch) square cake tin then spoon in the mixture. Bake in a preheated oven, 160°C, 325°F, Gas Mark 3 for 40-45 minutes or until firm and an inserted skewer comes out clean. Invert on a wire rack to cool.

Cut the cake in half horizontally and spread a thin layer of vanilla buttercream over the base. Add the top layer and spread with a thin layer of chocolate buttercream. Mark the top into 7 cm (3 inch) squares. Place the remaining chocolate and vanilla buttercream in 2 separate piping bags fitted with small star nozzles.

Use the chocolate buttercream to fill in the 4 outer corners and the centre square with small stars. Using the vanilla buttercream, fill in the remaining squares in the same way. Stand the chocolate triangles between the squares so that the points are uppermost.

Freezing: is recommended before decorating. When cold, wrap with tin foil and seal in a freezer bag. This will keep for up to 6 months. Defrost at room temperature for 2 hours and decorate as above.

MAKES 18 SLICES

Nutritional content per serving: Carbohydrate: 45 g   Fat: 17 g   Fibre: 1 g   Kilocalories: 338

ORANGE CHOCOLATE TEABREAD

300 g (10 oz) mixed dried fruit
50 g (2 oz) soft brown sugar
300 ml (½ pt) orange juice
1 egg, beaten
300 g (10 oz) self-raising flour
25 g (1 oz) drinking chocolate

Place the dried fruit, sugar and orange juice in a bowl. Cover and leave to soak for 4-5 hours.

Add the egg, flour and drinking chocolate and mix well. Spoon into a greased 1 kg (2 lb) loaf tin. Bake in a preheated oven, 180°C, 350°F, Gas Mark 4 for 45 minutes-1 hour or until an inserted skewer comes out clean. Leave to cool on a wire rack. Serve sliced and spread with butter.

Freezing: is recommended. When cold, wrap with tin foil and seal in a freezer bag. This will keep for up to 4 months. Defrost at room temperature for 2-3 hours.

MAKES 18-20 SLICES

Nutritional content per serving: Carbohydrate: 29 g   Fat: 1 g   Fibre: 2 g   Kilocalories: 125

Chequered Chocolate Cake; Orange Chocolate Teabread; Chocolate Chip Scones

CHOCOLATE CARROT AND RAISIN CAKE

THIS CAKE IMPROVES WITH KEEPING, SO MAKE IT A DAY OR TWO BEFORE SERVING AND STORE IN AN AIRTIGHT TIN. YOU WILL FIND THE CARROTS HELP KEEP IT MOIST. THE CURD CHEESE TOPPING IS OPTIONAL

150 g (5 oz) soft brown sugar
125 g (4 oz) sunflower margarine
175 g (6 oz) carrots, grated
125 g (4 oz) raisins
250 ml (8 fl oz) water
250 g (8 oz) wholemeal flour
25 g (1 oz) cocoa powder
½ teaspoon grated nutmeg
50 g (2 oz) ground almonds
1 teaspoon bicarbonate of soda
1 egg, beaten
TOPPING:
125 g (4 oz) skimmed milk soft cheese or
    curd cheese
125 g (4 oz) natural fromage frais
2 teaspoons clear honey
fine strands of orange rind

Place the sugar, margarine, carrots, raisins and water in a saucepan. Bring to the boil and boil for 5 minutes. Allow to cool.

Mix the dry ingredients in a bowl, then make a well in the centre. Add the egg and the contents of the saucepan, then beat well. Grease a 20 cm (8 inch) cake tin, line the base, and spoon in the mixture.

Bake in a preheated oven, 190°C, 375°F, Gas Mark 5 for 40-50 minutes or until firm and an inserted skewer comes out clean. Cool in the tin for 10 minutes then invert the cake on to a wire rack to cool completely.

Make the topping, if using. In a bowl, beat the cheese until softened and add the fromage frais and honey. Mix well. Spread over the cooled cake and decorate with fine strands of orange rind.

MAKES 12-15 SLICES

Nutritional content per serving:	Carbohydrate: 36 g	Fat: 12 g	Fibre: 4 g	Kilocalories: 275

GRANNY'S ICED CHOCOLATE SPONGE

175 g (6 oz) sunflower margarine
175 g (6 oz) caster sugar
2 eggs, beaten
200 g (7 oz) self-raising flour
25 g (1 oz) cocoa powder
6 tablespoons milk
FILLING AND TOPPING:
½ quantity Chocolate Buttercream Icing
    (see page 91)
1 quantity plain Glacé Icing (see page 91)
blue or green food colouring
walnut halves
chocolate buttons
glacé cherries, halved

Cream the margarine and sugar until pale and fluffy. Gradually beat in the eggs. Sift the flour and cocoa powder together and fold into the mixture with the milk to form a soft dropping consistency.

Grease 2 × 18 cm (7 inch) sandwich tins, line their bases and divide the mixture between them. Bake in a preheated oven, 180°C, 350°F, Gas Mark 4 for 20-25 minutes until risen and firm. Invert the cake layers on a wire rack to cool.

Sandwich the cake layers together with the chocolate buttercream icing. Add a few drops of blue or green food colouring to the glacé icing. Spread over the top of the sponge and decorate with walnuts, chocolate buttons and glacé cherries.

Freezing: is recommended before filling and decorating. When cold, wrap with tin foil and seal in a freezer bag. This will keep for up to 4 months. Defrost at room temperature for 2 hours. Fill and decorate as above.

MAKES 10-12 SLICES

Nutritional content per serving:	Carbohydrate: 60 g	Fat: 24 g	Fibre: 1 g	Kilocalories: 465

Chocolate Carrot and Raisin Cake; Walnut Brownies; Granny's Iced Chocolate Sponge

WALNUT BROWNIES

125 g (4 oz) sunflower margarine
250 g (8 oz) muscovado sugar
2 eggs
1 teaspoon vanilla flavouring
50 g (2 oz) plain flour
25 g (1 oz) cocoa powder
½ teaspoon baking powder
50 g (2 oz) walnuts, chopped
1 tablespoon milk
½ quantity Chocolate Fudge Frosting
  (see page 91)
walnut pieces to decorate

In a mixing bowl cream the margarine and sugar until pale and fluffy, then gradually beat in the eggs and vanilla flavouring.

Sift the flour, cocoa powder and baking powder together, then fold into the mixture with the chopped walnuts and milk. Grease an 18 cm (7 inch) square cake tin, line the base, spoon in the cake mixture and level the top.

Bake in a preheated oven, 180°C, 350°F, Gas Mark 4 for 30-35 minutes or until firm. Leave in the tin for 5 minutes, then invert on a wire rack to cool.

Spread the chocolate fudge frosting over the top of the cake, swirling with a fork. Decorate with walnut pieces and cut the cake into bars to serve.

Freezing: is recommended. Wrap in foil and seal in a freezer bag or place in a rigid container. These will keep for up to 3 months. Defrost at room temperature for 1-2 hours.

MAKES 15 BARS

Nutritional content per serving: Carbohydrate: 29 g   Fat: 13 g   Fibre: 0.5 g   Kilocalories: 231

CHOCOLATE-COATED TARTS

APRICOT JAM OR MARMALADE MAKE AN EQUALLY TASTY FILLING FOR THESE PLAIN CHOCOLATE TOPPED TARTS

FILLING:
75 g (3 oz) dried apricots
2 tablespoons water
12 teaspoons ginger preserve extra jam
SHORTCRUST PASTRY:
125 g (4 oz) plain flour
pinch of salt
25 g (1 oz) margarine
25 g (1 oz) lard
1 tablespoon water
TOPPING:
75 g (3 oz) plain chocolate, melted

Place the apricots and water in a bowl for the filling and leave to soak for 2 hours.

Meanwhile make the pastry. Sift the flour and salt into a bowl, then rub in the margarine and lard until the mixture resembles fine breadcrumbs. Add the water and mix to a stiff dough, then turn on to a floured board and knead until smooth. Roll out then, using a 7 cm (3 inch) fluted cutter, make circles to line 12 tartlet tins.

Drain the apricots, chop them finely and divide between the pastry cases. Top each with 1 teaspoon ginger preserve extra jam. Bake in a preheated oven, 190°C, 375°F, Gas Mark 5 for 15 minutes. Cool in the tin for 5 minutes, then transfer to a wire rack.

When completely cold, spread melted chocolate over the preserve and allow to set.

MAKES 12

Nutritional content per serving: Carbohydrate: 22 g   Fat: 5 g   Fibre: 2 g   Kilocalories: 141

CHOCOLATE STREUSEL CAKE

125 g (4 oz) self-raising flour
1 teaspoon baking powder
125 g (4 oz) sunflower margarine
2 eggs
TOPPING:
50 g (2 oz) plain flour
2 teaspoons cocoa powder
25 g (1 oz) butter
50 g (2 oz) demerara sugar
25 g (1 oz) white chocolate, grated

Place all the cake ingredients in a bowl and beat together to make a smooth batter. Grease an 18 cm (7 inch) square cake tin, line the base and spoon in the cake batter.

Make the topping. Sift the flour and cocoa powder into a bowl and rub in the butter until the mixture resembles fine breadcrumbs. Stir in the sugar and spoon the mixture over the cake batter.

Bake in a preheated oven, 180°C, 350°F, Gas Mark 4 for 30-40 minutes or until firm and an inserted skewer comes out clean. Leave in the tin for 5 minutes then transfer to a wire rack to cool completely. Decorate with grated white chocolate.

Freezing: is recommended. Place the cake in a rigid container or wrap in foil and seal in a freezer bag. This will keep for up to 3 months. Defrost at room temperature for 2 hours.

MAKES 10-12 SLICES

Nutritional content per serving: Carbohydrate: 21 g   Fat: 15 g   Fibre: 0.5 g   Kilocalories: 223

Chocolate Rock Buns; Chocolate-Coated Tarts; Chocolate Streusel Cake

CHOCOLATE ROCK BUNS

225 g (7 oz) self-raising flour
25 g (1 oz) cocoa powder
75 g (3 oz) caster sugar
75 g (3 oz) margarine
2 eggs, beaten
2 tablespoons milk
75 g (3 oz) plain or milk chocolate drops

Sift the flour and cocoa powder into a bowl and stir in the sugar. Rub in the margarine until the mixture resembles fine breadcrumbs. Add the eggs and milk, then mix to a stiff dough. Stir in the chocolate drops. Place spoonfuls of the mixture on greased baking sheets, allowing space for expansion. Bake in a preheated oven, 200°C, 400°F, Gas Mark 6 for 15-20 minutes. Leave to cool on a wire rack.

Freezing: is recommended. Wrap with tin foil and seal in a freezer bag. These will keep for up to 3 months. Defrost at room temperature for 1 hour.

MAKES 15-16

Nutritional content per serving: Carbohydrate: 20 g   Fat: 7 g   Fibre: 1 g   Kilocalories: 151

Marbled Meringues

MARBLED MERINGUES

2 egg whites
125 g (4 oz) caster sugar
50 g (2 oz) plain chocolate flavour cake
  covering, grated finely
1 × 142 ml (5 fl oz) carton double cream
2 small chocolate flakes, crumbled

Whisk the egg whites until stiff, then add the sugar 1 tablespoon at a time, whisking well. Fold in the grated chocolate.

Line a baking sheet with baking parchment. Place the meringue mixture in a large piping bag fitted with a 2 cm (¾ inch) plain or fluted nozzle and pipe 12 small oblong shapes of equal size on to the paper, allowing room for expansion. Bake in a preheated oven, 120°C, 250°F, Gas Mark ½ for 1 hour. Turn off the oven, leaving the meringues inside to cool gradually for about 8 hours or overnight.

Whip the double cream until thick and fold in the chocolate flakes. Use to sandwich the meringues together. Serve immediately.

MAKES 6

Nutritional content per serving: Carbohydrate: 32 g   Fat: 16 g   Kilocalories: 270

WHOLEMEAL CHOCOLATE FUDGE CAKE

25 g (1 oz) cocoa powder
3 teaspoons instant coffee granules
125 ml (4 fl oz) hot water
125 g (4 oz) sunflower margarine
125 g (4 oz) soft brown sugar
3 eggs, beaten
75 g (3 oz) plain chocolate, melted
250 g (8 oz) self-raising wholemeal flour
FROSTING:
1 × 227 g (8 oz) carton skimmed milk soft
  cheese or curd cheese
75 g (3 oz) plain chocolate, melted
TO DECORATE:
grated chocolate
Chocolate Caraque (see page 7)

In a measuring jug or bowl mix the cocoa powder and coffee granules with the hot water, then leave to cool.

Cream the margarine and sugar in a mixing bowl until light and fluffy, then gradually add the eggs, beating well after each addition. Stir in the prepared coffee mixture and the melted chocolate, then fold in the flour and mix well.

Grease a 20 cm (8 inch) cake tin, line the base and spoon in the mixture. Bake in a preheated oven, 180°C, 350°F, Gas Mark 4 for 30-40 minutes or until firm. Invert on a wire rack to cool.

Cut the cake in half horizontally. To make the frosting beat the cheese until softened, add the melted chocolate and beat well. Use half to sandwich the cake layers together and spread the rest over the top, using a dampened palette knife to give a smooth finish.

Decorate with alternate bands of grated chocolate and caraque. Cover the cake and refrigerate until required.

MAKES 8-10 SLICES

Nutritional content per serving:	Carbohydrate: 52 g	Fat: 23 g	Fibre: 3 g	Kilocalories: 436

Wholemeal Chocolate Fudge Cake

MARBLE CAKE

125 g (4 oz) sunflower margarine
125 g (4 oz) caster sugar
2 eggs, beaten
125 g (4 oz) self-raising flour, sifted
2 teaspoons cold milk
pink food colouring
green food colouring
2 teaspoons cocoa powder
2 drops vanilla flavouring
½ quantity Chocolate Glacé Icing
    (see page 91)
chocolate sugar strands

Place the margarine, sugar, eggs, flour and milk in a bowl and beat together for 2-3 minutes. Divide between 3 bowls. Tint the first with pink colouring and the second with green. Stir the cocoa powder and vanilla flavouring into the third bowl. Mix the contents of each bowl well, then place alternate spoonfuls of each mixture into a greased fluted 18 cm (7 inch) cake tin. Knock the tin on a level surface to remove air pockets then level the top.

Bake in a preheated oven, 180°C, 350°F, Gas Mark 4 for 30-35 minutes or until an inserted skewer comes out clean. Invert on a wire rack to cool. Decorate with glacé icing and chocolate sugar strands.

MAKES 8-10 SLICES

Nutritional content per serving: Carbohydrate: 31 g   Fat: 16 g   Kilocalories: 269

CHOCOLATE BUTTERCREAM SPONGE

A CLASSIC RECIPE WHICH CAN BE USED AS A BASIS FOR MORE ELABORATELY DECORATED CAKES (SEE THE CHAPTER ON NOVELTY CAKES)

175 g (6 oz) butter, softened
175 g (6 oz) caster sugar
3 eggs, beaten
150 g (5 oz) self-raising flour
25 g (1 oz) cocoa powder
1 tablespoon milk
3 drops vanilla flavouring
1 quantity Chocolate Buttercream Icing
    (see page 91)
chocolate buttons, halved, to decorate

In a bowl cream the butter and sugar together until pale and fluffy. Add the beaten eggs, a little at a time, beating well after each addition.

Sift the flour and cocoa powder together. Fold half the mixture into the mixing bowl, add the milk, then fold in the remaining flour with the vanilla flavouring. Mix gently yet thoroughly. Grease 2 × 18 cm (7 inch) sandwich tins, line the bases, then divide the cake mixture between them. Level both mixtures with a palette knife and bake in a preheated oven, 190°C, 375°F, Gas Mark 5 for 20 minutes or until risen and an inserted skewer comes out clean. Leave in the tins for 5 minutes, then invert the cakes on a wire rack to cool.

Sandwich the cake layers together with half the buttercream icing. Use most of the remaining buttercream to cover the top of the cake, reserving some to pipe rosettes around the edge. Decorate with chocolate buttons.

Freezing: is recommended before or after decorating. Freeze the decorated cake without wrapping until hard, then wrap with tin foil and seal in a freezer bag, or wrap and seal the cooled sponge cake layers before decorating. Both will keep for up to 3 months. Defrost the whole cake at room temperature for 3-4 hours and the sponge cake layers for 1-2 hours.

MAKES 8-10 SLICES

Nutritional content per serving: Carbohydrate: 73 g   Fat: 36 g   Fibre: 1 g   Kilocalories: 618

FAMILY CAKES   69

CHOCOLATE BRAN MUFFINS

125 g (4 oz) wholemeal flour
75 g (3 oz) high-fibre bran cereal, crushed
2 teaspoons baking powder
1 tablespoon cocoa powder
1 tablespoon drinking chocolate
25 g (1 oz) soft brown sugar
1 egg
4 tablespoons sunflower oil
250 ml (8 fl oz) milk

Combine the first 6 ingredients in a mixing bowl. Mix thoroughly, then make a well in the centre.

In a jug or bowl, whisk the egg and oil together and add the milk. Pour into the well and gradually incorporate with the dry ingredients. Beat well. Spoon into 12 greased deep bun tins or 18 shallow tartlet tins. Bake in a preheated oven, 200°C, 400°F, Gas Mark 6 for 25-35 minutes or until risen and firm. Serve warm, spread with butter.

Freezing: is recommended. Wrap the cooled muffins with tin foil, seal in a freezer bag and freeze. These will keep for up to 2 months. Defrost at room temperature for 1 hour.

MAKES 12-18

Nutritional content per serving:	Carbohydrate: 16 g	Fat: 7 g	Fibre: 2 g	Kilocalories: 135

Marble Cake; Chocolate Buttercream Sponge; Chocolate Bran Muffins

YOGURT CHOCOLATE CAKE

150 ml (¼ pint) sunflower oil
1 × 125 g (4.4 oz) carton chocolate yogurt
5 tablespoons golden syrup
175 g (6 oz) caster sugar
3 eggs
250 g (8 oz) self-raising flour
25 g (1 oz) cocoa powder
½ teaspoon bicarbonate of soda
½ teaspoon salt
TOPPING:
125 g (4 oz) plain chocolate
25 g (1 oz) butter
2 teaspoons milk
White Chocolate Caraque (see page 7)

Place the oil, yogurt, golden syrup, sugar and eggs in a mixing bowl and beat well. Sift the flour, cocoa powder, bicarbonate of soda and salt into the bowl and mix well.

Grease a 20 cm (8 inch) cake tin, line the base and pour in the mixture. Bake in a preheated oven, 160°C, 325°F, Gas Mark 3 for 1½-1¾ hours or until an inserted skewer comes out clean. Invert on a wire rack to cool.

Make the topping. Place the chocolate, butter and milk in a heatproof bowl over a saucepan of gently simmering water. Stir until the chocolate has melted. Spread the mixture over the cooled cake and make patterns with a fork. Decorate with chocolate caraque.

Freezing: is recommended before spreading on the topping and decorating. When cold, wrap with tin foil and seal in a freezer bag, then freeze. This will keep for up to 4 months. Defrost at room temperature for 2 hours.

MAKES 8-10 SLICES

Nutritional content per serving:	Carbohydrate: 72 g	Fat: 30 g	Fibre: 1 g	Kilocalories: 573

BANANA CHOCOLATE SLICES

THE BANANAS IN THIS CAKE MAKE IT MOIST BUT NOT TOO SWEET

50 g (2 oz) sunflower margarine
50 g (2 oz) soft brown sugar
2 large ripe bananas, mashed
2 tablespoons cocoa powder
1 tablespoon drinking chocolate
1 × 150 g (5.2 oz) carton natural yogurt
1 egg, beaten
175 g (6 oz) wholemeal flour
1½ teaspoons baking powder
½ teaspoon bicarbonate of soda
25 g (1 oz) crunchy oat cereal
1 tablespoon demerara sugar

In a mixing bowl, cream the margarine with the soft brown sugar until pale and fluffy. Beat in the bananas, cocoa powder, drinking chocolate, yogurt and egg. Mix well, then stir in the flour, baking powder and bicarbonate of soda.

Grease an 18 cm (7 inch) square tin, line the base, and spoon in the mixture. Level the top and sprinkle with the crunchy oat cereal and demerara sugar.

Bake in a preheated oven, 180°C, 350°F, Gas Mark 4 for 40-45 minutes or until just firm. Leave in the tin for 5 minutes then invert on to a wire rack to cool completely. Cut into slices to serve.

Freezing: is recommended. When cold wrap with tin foil and seal in a freezer bag. These will keep for up to 3 months. Defrost at room temperature for 1-2 hours.

MAKES 18-20

Nutritional content per serving:	Carbohydrate: 23 g	Fat: 5 g	Fibre: 2 g	Kilocalories: 149

Banana Chocolate Slices; Yogurt Chocolate Cake; No-Cook Chocolate Cake

NO-COOK CHOCOLATE CAKE

125 g (4 oz) butter
2 tablespoons golden syrup
1 tablespoon milk
125 g (4 oz) plain chocolate, melted
250 g (8 oz) rustic biscuits, crushed
25 g (1 oz) sultanas
25 g (1 oz) raisins
50 g (2 oz) glacé cherries, chopped
40 g (1½ oz) unsalted peanuts, chopped
½ quantity Chocolate Fudge Frosting
   (see page 91)

Place the butter, golden syrup and milk in a large heatproof bowl over a saucepan of gently simmering water. Stir until the butter has melted. Remove from the heat, stir in the melted chocolate and crushed biscuits and mix well. Add the sultanas, raisins, cherries and peanuts. Mix well.

Spoon into a greased 500 g (1 lb) loaf tin with the base lined. Press down well and chill for 1-2 hours.

Turn the cake on to a serving plate, remove the lining paper, then spread a thick layer of chocolate fudge frosting over the top of the cake and make swirling patterns with a palette knife.

Microwave: Cook the butter, syrup and milk in a bowl on Full Power for 1 minute.

MAKES 16 SLICES

Nutritional content per serving: Carbohydrate: 33 g   Fat: 15 g   Fibre: 1 g   Kilocalories: 265

BISCUITS

SERVE A CHOICE OF CHOCOLATE-FLAVOURED BISCUITS AT A COFFEE MORNING OR AS A TREAT WITH AFTERNOON TEA. IF THEY'RE NOT ALL EATEN AT ONCE, KEEP IN AN AIRTIGHT CONTAINER FOR UP TO 1 WEEK OR, IF YOU WANT TO STORE THEM FOR LONGER, FREEZE IN A RIGID CONTAINER.

COCONUT CHOCOLATE CRISPIES

125 g (4 oz) milk chocolate, broken
2 tablespoons milk
2 tablespoons golden syrup
125 g (4 oz) rice pops
75 g (3 oz) desiccated coconut

Place the chocolate, milk and golden syrup in a bowl over a pan of simmering water. Stir until the chocolate has melted. Add the cereal and coconut and mix well. Arrange 20 paper cake cases on a baking sheet and divide the mixture between them. Leave to set.

MAKES 20

Nutritional content per serving:	Carbohydrate: 9 g	Fat: 4 g	Fibre: 2 g	Kilocalories: 81

CHOCOLATE CHIP SESAME FLAPJACKS

75 g (3 oz) sunflower margarine
3 tablespoons golden syrup
3 tablespoons plain chocolate drops
1 tablespoon sesame seeds
175 g (6 oz) porridge oats

Place the margarine and syrup in a saucepan and heat gently until the margarine has melted. Remove from the heat and add the chocolate drops, sesame seeds and oats and mix well. Grease an 18 cm (7 inch) square cake tin, line the base then press in the mixture.

Bake in a preheated oven, 160°C, 325°F, Gas Mark 3 for 25 minutes. Leave in the tin for 10 minutes then cut into 9-12 flapjacks and transfer to a wire rack to cool completely.

Microwave: In a deep bowl or jug, cook the margarine and syrup on Full Power for 1 minute.

MAKES 9-12

Nutritional content per serving:	Carbohydrate: 23 g	Fat: 11 g	Fibre: 1 g	Kilocalories: 191

CHOCOLATE TOP GINGERS

175 g (6 oz) wholemeal flour
50 g (2 oz) porridge oats
½ teaspoon bicarbonate of soda
1 teaspoon cream of tartar
2 teaspoons ground ginger
175 g (6 oz) margarine
175 g (6 oz) demerara sugar
200 g (7 oz) plain chocolate flavour cake
  covering, melted

Place the flour, porridge oats, bicarbonate of soda, cream of tartar and ground ginger in a bowl. Rub in the margarine until the mixture resembles fine breadcrumbs. Stir in the sugar and press into a greased 28 × 18 cm (11 × 7 inch) Swiss roll tin.

Bake in a preheated oven, 160°C, 325°F, Gas Mark 3 for 30 minutes or until lightly browned. Cool in the tin, then cover with the melted chocolate cake covering. When set, cut into fingers.

Freezing: is recommended. When cold, place in a rigid airtight container. These will keep for up to 3 months. Defrost at room temperature for 2 hours.

MAKES 20

Nutritional content per serving:	Carbohydrate: 24 g	Fat: 10 g	Fibre: 1 g	Kilocalories: 190

Chocolate Chip Sesame Flapjacks; Chocolate Top Gingers; Coconut Chocolate Crispies

Chocolate nut cookies

250 g (8 oz) plain flour
1 teaspoon baking powder
125 g (4 oz) sunflower margarine
175 g (6 oz) caster sugar
50 g (2 oz) plain or milk chocolate drops
25 g (1 oz) chopped nuts
1 teaspoon vanilla flavouring
1 egg, beaten

Sift the flour and baking powder into a bowl and rub in the margarine until the mixture resembles fine breadcrumbs. Stir in the sugar, chocolate drops and nuts. Add the vanilla flavouring and egg, then mix to a stiff dough.

Turn on to a floured surface and knead, then roll into a long sausage. Wrap in a sheet of foil, twisting the ends to seal. Roll the foil-wrapped sausage backwards and forwards to form an even-shaped roll about 5 cm (2 inch) thick. Place in the refrigerator for several hours or overnight.

For baking, cut the number of biscuits required and space out on greased baking sheets. Cook in a preheated oven, 190°C, 375°F, Gas Mark 5 for 10-12 minutes. Leave on the baking sheet for 5 minutes, then transfer to a wire rack to cool completely. Store in an airtight container. The roll of uncooked dough will keep in the refrigerator for 1 week.

MAKES 50-60

Nutritional content per serving: Carbohydrate: 8 g   Fat: 3 g   Fibre: 5 g   Kilocalories: 59

Chocolate date and oat fingers

175 g (6 oz) chopped dates
3 tablespoons water
50 g (2 oz) plain chocolate, melted
125 ml (4 fl oz) sunflower oil
1 tablespoon clear honey
25 g (1 oz) demerara sugar
125 g (4 oz) porridge oats
125 g (4 oz) wholemeal flour

Place the dates and water in a saucepan. Simmer gently for 5 minutes until the dates are soft. Add the melted chocolate to the dates, mix well and set aside.

Mix the oil with the honey in a bowl. Add the sugar, oats and flour and stir thoroughly.

Grease an 18 cm (7 inch) square cake tin, line its base and place half the mixture in it. Press down well, then spread with the chocolate and date mixture. Top with the remaining oat mixture, pressing it down well. Bake in a preheated oven, 190°C, 375°F, Gas Mark 5 for 20-25 minutes or until golden. Cool in the tin for 5 minutes, cut into 12 fingers, then leave to cool completely in the tin. Store in an airtight container.

Microwave: In a bowl, cook the dates and water on Full Power for 1 minute.

Freezing: is recommended. When cold, wrap in foil and seal in a freezer bag. These will keep for up to 3 months. Defrost at room temperature for 2 hours.

MAKES 12

Nutritional content per serving: Carbohydrate: 30 g   Fat: 13 g   Fibre: 3 g   Kilocalories: 238

Chocolate Nut Cookies; Chocolate Date and Oat Fingers; Chocolate Crunch Wedges

CHOCOLATE CRUNCH WEDGES

75 g (3 oz) butter
2 tablespoons golden syrup
1 tablespoon soft brown sugar
1 tablespoon cocoa powder
250 g (8 oz) digestive biscuits, crushed
50 g (2 oz) raisins

Place the butter, golden syrup, sugar and cocoa powder in a saucepan and heat gently until the butter has melted.

Stir in the biscuit crumbs and raisins. Press the mixture into a greased 20 cm (8 inch) flan ring or loose-bottomed tin. Chill in the refrigerator until firm, then cut into wedges.

Microwave: The first 4 ingredients may be cooked in a bowl on Full Power for 2 minutes, stirring once.

Freezing: is recommended. Place in a rigid airtight container or wrap in foil and seal in a freezer bag. These will keep for up to 4 months. Defrost at room temperature for 1-2 hours.

MAKES 12-16

Nutritional content per serving: Carbohydrate: 21 g   Fat: 10 g   Fibre: 1 g   Kilocalories: 173

CHOCOLATE VIENNESE BISCUITS

125 g (4 oz) sunflower margarine
25 g (1 oz) icing sugar
125 g (4 oz) plain flour
1 tablespoon cocoa powder
1 tablespoon drinking chocolate
½ teaspoon vanilla flavouring
TO DECORATE:
75 g (3 oz) plain chocolate, melted
icing sugar, sifted

In a mixing bowl, cream the margarine with the sugar until pale and fluffy. Sift the flour, cocoa powder and drinking chocolate into the bowl and mix well. Stir in the vanilla flavouring.

Spoon the mixture into a large piping bag fitted with a 1.5 cm (¾ inch) fluted nozzle. Pipe 18–20 fingers 7 cm (3 inches) long on to greased baking sheets, allowing room for expansion.

Bake in a preheated oven, 190°C, 375°F, Gas Mark 5 for 15-20 minutes. Leave on the baking sheet for 5 minutes, then transfer to a wire rack to cool completely.

Dip both ends of each biscuit in the melted chocolate and place on greaseproof paper to set. Arrange the biscuits in a line. Carefully mask the chocolate-coated ends with strips of greaseproof paper, then dredge the centres with sifted icing sugar.

Freezing: is recommended before decorating. When cold, pack the biscuits in a rigid airtight container. These will keep for up to 4 months. Defrost at room temperature for 2 hours.

MAKES 18-20

Nutritional content per serving:	Carbohydrate: 11 g	Fat: 7 g	Fibre: 0.5 g	Kilocalories: 111

Chocolate Viennese Biscuits

Florentines

FLORENTINES

A CHOCOLATE COOKBOOK WOULD NOT BE COMPLETE WITHOUT A RECIPE FOR THESE DELICIOUS FRUITY BISCUITS

50 g (2 oz) butter
50 g (2 oz) caster sugar
25 g (1 oz) plain or wholemeal flour
40 g (1½ oz) glacé cherries, chopped finely
25 g (1 oz) stem ginger, chopped finely
25 g (1 oz) flaked almonds
25 g (1 oz) mixed peel, chopped finely
125 g (4 oz) plain chocolate, melted

Line a large baking sheet with 2 layers of baking parchment and then set it aside.

Place the butter and sugar in a heatproof bowl over a saucepan of gently simmering water. Stir until the butter has melted, then remove from the heat and add the flour. Mix until smooth, then stir in the glacé cherries, stem ginger, flaked almonds and mixed peel.

Place spoonfuls of the mixture well apart on the baking sheet. Bake in a preheated oven, 180°C, 350°F, Gas Mark 4 for 8-10 minutes until golden. Allow to cool for 10 minutes then, using a palette knife, carefully transfer to a wire rack to cool completely.

Spread the melted chocolate over one side of each florentine and mark lines with a fork if wished. Leave to harden.

Microwave: Cook the florentines in two batches on baking parchment for 2½ minutes on Medium Power.

MAKES 10-12

Nutritional content per serving: Carbohydrate: 20 g   Fat: 9 g   Fibre: 1 g   Kilocalories: 164

CHOCOLATE LEMON DIGESTIVES

75 g (3 oz) wholemeal flour
pinch of salt
½ teaspoon baking powder
40 g (1½ oz) medium oatmeal
40 g (1½ oz) butter
25 g (1 oz) soft brown sugar
finely grated rind of ½ lemon
3 tablespoons milk
TOPPING:
1½ teaspoons lemon juice
50 g (2 oz) plain or milk chocolate, melted

Place the flour, salt, baking powder and oatmeal in a mixing bowl. Rub in the butter until the mixture resembles fine breadcrumbs. Stir in the sugar and lemon rind. Add the milk and mix to a stiff biscuit dough. Turn on to a floured board and knead well. Roll out to a circle just under 5 mm (¼ inch) thick.

Using a 7 cm (3 inch) plain cutter, cut out 12 biscuits, rolling the dough again as necessary. Place the biscuits, allowing room for expansion, on a greased baking sheet.

Prick well and bake in a preheated oven, 190°C, 375°F, Gas Mark 5 for 15-20 minutes or until lightly browned. Transfer to a wire rack to cool.

Stir the lemon juice into the melted chocolate and spread over the biscuits. Mark lines over the chocolate before it sets.

Freezing: is recommended. Freeze in a rigid airtight container. These will keep for up to 2 months. Defrost at room temperature for 2 hours.

MAKES 12

Nutritional content per serving:	Carbohydrate: 12 g	Fat: 4 g	Fibre: 1 g	Kilocalories: 91

CHOCOLATE SHORTBREAD

FOR A CRISPER SHORTBREAD OMIT THE SEMOLINA AND REPLACE WITH 20 G (¾ OZ) PLAIN FLOUR

125 g (4 oz) butter, softened
50 g (2 oz) caster sugar
140 g (4½ oz) plain flour
20 g (¾ oz) cocoa powder
20 g (¾ oz) semolina
sifted icing sugar or 125 g (4 oz) white
   chocolate, melted, to decorate

In a mixing bowl, cream the butter with the sugar until pale and fluffy. Sift the flour and cocoa powder together and work into the butter mixture with the semolina. Press into a greased 18 cm (7 inch) shortbread mould or sandwich tin and flatten the top. Use a fork to press down the edges.

Bake in a preheated oven, 160°C, 325°F, Gas Mark 3 for 30-35 minutes. Mark into 8-10 pieces and leave to cool in the tin for 10 minutes, then transfer to a wire rack to cool completely.

Dust with sifted icing sugar or spread with the melted white chocolate. Cut into wedges to serve.

Freezing: is recommended. When cold, pack the shortbread into a rigid airtight container or wrap in foil and seal in a freezer bag. It will keep for up to 4 months. Defrost at room temperature for 2 hours.

MAKES 8-10

Nutritional content per serving:	Carbohydrate: 25 g	Fat: 14 g	Fibre: 1 g	Kilocalories: 225

Chocolate Lemon Digestives; Coconut Caramel Squares; Chocolate Shortbread

COCONUT CARAMEL SQUARES

75 g (3 oz) butter, melted
25 g (1 oz) drinking chocolate
125 g (4 oz) digestive biscuits, crushed
25 g (1 oz) desiccated coconut
TOPPING:
1 × 397 g (14 oz) can condensed milk
25 g (1 oz) butter
2 tablespoons golden syrup
1 teaspoon vanilla flavouring
50 g (2 oz) plain chocolate flavour cake
    covering, broken
White Chocolate Curls (see page 7) to
    decorate

In a bowl, mix the butter with the drinking chocolate, crushed biscuits and coconut. Press into a greased 18 cm (7 inch) square cake tin.

Place all the topping ingredients in a saucepan and heat, stirring until the chocolate and butter have melted and the liquid begins to boil. Boil for 4 minutes, stirring vigorously, then pour over the biscuit base and leave in a cool place to set. Cut into 16 squares and store in an airtight container in the refrigerator until required. To serve, decorate with white chocolate curls.

Freezing: is recommended. Pack in a rigid airtight container with foil or greaseproof paper between the layers. These will keep for up to 2 months. Defrost at room temperature for 2 hours.

MAKES 16

Nutritional content per serving:	Carbohydrate: 24 g	Fat: 11 g	Fibre: 1 g	Kilocalories: 200

NOVELTY CAKES AND SWEETS

THEME CAKES IN THE FORM OF RABBITS, HEDGEHOGS, CASTLES AND CLOCKS ARE ALWAYS GREAT FAVOURITES WITH CHILDREN, NEVER FAILING TO PLEASE. SWEETS, WHICH ARE QUICKER TO MAKE, WILL BE GREETED WITH EQUAL ENTHUSIASM, AND MAKE EXCELLENT GIFTS IF WRAPPED IN PRETTY BOXES.

CHOCOLATE BUTTERFLIES

125 g (4 oz) self-raising flour
pinch of salt
25 g (1 oz) drinking chocolate
1 teaspoon cocoa powder
50 g (2 oz) butter
50 g (2 oz) caster sugar
1 egg, beaten
3 tablespoons milk
3 drops vanilla flavouring
TO DECORATE:
½ quantity Vanilla Buttercream Icing
  (see page 91)
Chocolate Triangles (see page 7)
grated chocolate

Sift the flour, salt, drinking chocolate and cocoa powder into a mixing bowl. Rub in the butter until the mixture resembles fine breadcrumbs. Stir in the sugar and make a well in the centre. Add the egg, milk and vanilla flavouring, then mix well.

Spoon the mixture into 12-14 paper cake cases placed on a baking sheet or in patty tins. Bake in a preheated oven, 190°C, 375°F, Gas Mark 5 for 15-20 minutes.

Cool the cakes on a wire rack. Pipe whirls of vanilla buttercream around the top of the cakes. Arrange the chocolate triangles on top to resemble wings. Sprinkle grated chocolate between the wings.

MAKES 12-14

Nutritional content per serving:	Carbohydrate: 28 g	Fat: 10 g	Fibre: 0.5 g	Kilocalories: 204

MARSHMALLOW NUT FUDGE

2 tablespoons milk
125 g (4 oz) marshmallows, chopped
50 g (2 oz) butter
50 g (2 oz) granulated or caster sugar
1 tablespoon drinking chocolate
125 g (4 oz) icing sugar, sifted
25 g (1 oz) chopped hazelnuts, toasted

Place 1 tablespoon of the milk and the marshmallows in a saucepan. Heat gently until the marshmallows have melted. Spoon into a bowl and set aside.

Add the remaining milk to the saucepan with the butter, sugar and drinking chocolate. Heat gently, stirring until the butter has melted and the sugar has dissolved. Boil for 5 minutes. Remove from the heat and stir in the marshmallow mixture, icing sugar and hazelnuts. Spread in a greased 15 cm (6 inch) square tin. When hard, cut into squares.

MAKES 25-30 SQUARES

Nutritional content per serving:	Carbohydrate: 11 g	Fat: 2 g	Kilocalories: 62

QUICK CHOCOLATE LOG

1 Mocha Swiss Roll (see page 59)
1 quantity Chocolate Buttercream Icing
  (see page 91)
sifted icing sugar
robin and holly decoration

Place the mocha Swiss roll on a board and cover with the buttercream. Create a bark effect by making horizontal lines along the log and circular lines at either end. Transfer the log to a serving dish and dust with icing sugar. Decorate with holly and a robin.

MAKES 8-10 SLICES

Nutritional content per serving:	Carbohydrate: 70 g	Fat: 23 g	Fibre: 0.5 g	Kilocalories: 489

Marshmallow Nut Fudge; Chocolate Butterflies; Quick Chocolate Log.

CHOCOLATE COCONUT ICE

300 ml (½ pint) milk
1 kg (2 lb) granulated sugar
250 g (8 oz) desiccated coconut
1 teaspoon cocoa powder

Place the milk and sugar in a saucepan and heat gently, stirring, until the sugar dissolves. Bring to the boil, cover the pan and boil for 8-10 minutes without stirring until a sugar thermometer reads 115-116°C, 238°–240°F or when a little of the mixture dropped into a cup of water forms a soft ball.

Remove the pan from the heat and add the coconut, beating well until thick and creamy. Pour half the mixture into a greased 20 cm (8 inch) square tin.

Quickly beat the cocoa into the remaining mixture and spread over the white layer. When set cut into squares or bars.

MAKES ABOUT 60 SMALL PIECES

Nutritional content per serving: Carbohydrate: 18 g   Fat: 3 g   Fibre: 1 g   Kilocalories: 94

CHOCOLATE RABBIT

175 g (6 oz) plain flour
25 g (1 oz) cocoa powder
1 teaspoon baking powder
1 teaspoon bicarbonate of soda
pinch of salt
125 g (4 oz) caster sugar
75 g (3 oz) sunflower margarine
150 ml (¼ pint) milk
2 eggs
1 tablespoon black treacle
TO DECORATE AND FINISH:
2 quantities Chocolate Buttercream Icing
   (see page 91)
125 g (4 oz) white marzipan
pink food colouring
orange food colouring
angelica
1 liquorice sweet
cocktail sticks

Sift the first 5 ingredients into a mixing bowl, then add the sugar, margarine, milk, eggs and treacle. Beat well for 2-3 minutes. Grease and then line the base of a 20 cm (8 inch) round cake tin and spoon in the mixture. Bake in a preheated oven, 160°C, 325°F, Gas Mark 3 for 30-40 minutes or until firm and an inserted skewer comes out clean. Invert on a wire rack to cool.

Cut the cake in half vertically to form 2 semi-circles. Sandwich together with one quarter of the buttercream, then stand the cake on end, with the rounded side uppermost. Trim one end to form a snout. Cover the cake with the rest of the buttercream, using it to shape the snout – smooth this area with a palette knife. Roughen the buttercream elsewhere on the rabbit. Place on a cake board.

Roll about one third of the marzipan into a ball for the tail. Mark with a fork to give a fluffy appearance, then attach to the back of the rabbit. Add a few drops of pink and orange food colouring to the remaining marzipan and knead until evenly coloured. Roll a small piece into a ball to form the nose. Place this at the end of the snout and flatten slightly. Shape 2 equal-sized pieces of marzipan into rabbit ears about 5 cm (2 inches) long. Press into position on the head.

Add a few more drops of orange colouring to the marzipan. Knead well and form into a carrot. Stick thin strips of angelica into the wider end to form the greenery. Place it beside the rabbit.

Cut the liquorice sweet in half and use to make eyes. Break the cocktail sticks in half and place in position for whiskers.

MAKES 15-20 PIECES

Nutritional content per serving: Carbohydrate: 62 g   Fat: 20 g   Fibre: 1 g   Kilocalories: 432

Chocolate Coconut Ice; Simple Chocolate Fudge; Chocolate Rabbit

SIMPLE CHOCOLATE FUDGE

25 g (1 oz) butter
50 g (2 oz) plain chocolate, broken
2 tablespoons single cream
½ teaspoon vanilla flavouring
250 g (8 oz) icing sugar, sifted

Place the butter and chocolate in a heatproof bowl and place over a saucepan of simmering water. Stir until the chocolate has melted.

Stir in the single cream and vanilla flavouring. Gradually work in the icing sugar and mix well. Spoon into a small, greased shallow tray and leave to set. Cut into squares and store in an airtight container until required.

Microwave: Melt the butter and chocolate together in a bowl on Full Power for 1 ½ minutes.

MAKES 20 SQUARES

Nutritional content per serving: Carbohydrate: 15 g   Fat: 2 g   Kilocalories: 75

Chocolate Raisin Fudge; Keyboard Cake; Chocolate Peppermint Creams

CHOCOLATE RAISIN FUDGE

300 ml (½ pint) milk
125 g (4 oz) plain chocolate, broken
875 g (1 lb 12 oz) golden granulated sugar
125 g (4 oz) butter
50 g (2 oz) raisins
2 teaspoons vanilla flavouring

Place the milk and chocolate in a saucepan and heat gently until the chocolate has melted. Add the sugar and butter and continue to heat, stirring, until the sugar has dissolved.

Bring to the boil, cover and boil for 2 minutes. Remove the lid and boil without stirring for 10-15 minutes or until a sugar thermometer reads 115-116°C, 238°-240°F or when a little of the mixture dropped into a cup of cold water forms a soft ball.

Remove from the heat, stir in the raisins and vanilla flavouring. Cool for 5-10 minutes. Beat the fudge until it loses its gloss, then spoon into a greased 18 cm (7 inch) square tin. When set cut into neat squares.

MAKES ABOUT 50 PIECES

Nutritional content per serving: Carbohydrate: 21 g   Fat: 3 g   Kilocalories: 107

KEYBOARD CAKE

250 g (8 oz) butter
250 g (8 oz) caster sugar
4 eggs, beaten
190 g (6½ oz) self-raising flour
3 tablespoons cocoa powder
1½ tablespoons milk
4 drops vanilla flavouring
TO DECORATE AND FINISH:
2 quantities Chocolate Buttercream Icing
  (see page 91)
8 sponge fingers
liquorice strips
small liquorice allsorts
birthday candles as required

Make the sponge cake, following the instructions for Chocolate Buttercream Sponge (see page 68), but using the ingredients in quantities listed here. Grease and then line the base of a 30 × 23 cm (12 × 9 inch) roasting tin and spoon in the mixture. Level the top and make a slight hollow in the centre. Bake in a preheated oven, 190°C, 375°F, Gas Mark 5 for 30-40 minutes or until risen and an inserted skewer comes out clean. Invert on a wire rack to cool.

Place the cake on a board and trim the edges. Cut a strip 6 cm (2½ inches) wide from the long side of the cake. Cut the larger piece of cake in half horizontally and sandwich the 2 halves together with a thin layer of buttercream. Turn the strip on end and attach with buttercream to the back of the cake. Cover the whole cake with the remaining buttercream.

Place the sponge fingers on the cake to make the white keys. Cut the liquorice strips and position between the sponge fingers for the black keys. Cut sections from small liquorice allsorts and position to the side and behind the keys for buttons and controls.

Position birthday candles along the back section. Serve the cake on a foil-lined tray or rectangular cake board.

MAKES 24-28 PIECES

Nutritional content per serving: Carbohydrate: 44 g   Fat: 19 g   Fibre: 0.5 g   Kilocalories: 354

CHOCOLATE PEPPERMINT CREAMS

25 g (1 oz) butter
1 tablespoon single cream
250 g (8 oz) icing sugar
2 teaspoons cocoa powder
½ teaspoon peppermint flavouring
sifted icing sugar for dusting

Place the butter and cream in a heatproof bowl and place over a saucepan of gently simmering water. Stir until the butter has melted.

Sift the icing sugar and cocoa powder together, then work into the butter and cream with the peppermint flavouring. When cool enough to handle, knead until smooth, then turn on to a surface lightly dusted with sifted icing sugar.

Divide the mixture into 2 and roll each piece to a cylinder about 15 cm (6 inches) long. Cut each into 15 pieces and arrange in individual sweet cases or a lined box. Store the peppermints in an airtight container until required.

MAKES 30 PIECES

Nutritional content per serving: Carbohydrate: 9 g   Fat: 1 g   Kilocalories: 41

CHOCOLATE HEDGEHOGS

125 g (4 oz) butter, softened

125 g (4 oz) caster sugar

2 eggs, beaten

75 g (3 oz) self-raising flour

25 g (1 oz) cocoa powder

1 tablespoon milk

2 drops vanilla flavouring

1 quantity Chocolate Buttercream Icing
(see page 91)

TO DECORATE:

1 × 113 g (4 oz) tub chocolate-flavoured
sugar strands

1 × 120 g (4 oz) packet chocolate mint
sticks

36 silver balls

5 liquorice pieces from 1 packet of small
liquorice allsorts

Make the sponge following the method for Chocolate Buttercream Sponge (see page 68), but using the ingredients quantities listed here. Spoon the cake mixture into 18 greased shallow rounded patty tins. Bake in a preheated oven, 180°C, 350°F, Gas Mark 4 for 15-18 minutes or until risen and firm. Leave in the tin for 5 minutes, then transfer the cakes to a wire rack to cool completely.

Slice off the top of each cake to make it flat, then place upside down on a board. Cover each cake with buttercream, shaping it to form a snout. Sprinkle the hedgehogs with chocolate sugar strands. Cut the chocolate mint sticks into 1.5 cm (¾ inch) pieces and insert into the icing to make spikes. Place 2 silver balls above each snout for eyes. Cut each liquorice piece into 4, using each round as a nose. Transfer the hedgehogs to a serving plate.

MAKES 18

Nutritional content per serving: Carbohydrate: 41 g   Fat: 15 g   Fibre: 0.5 g   Kilocalories: 296

Chocolate Hedgehogs

Castle Cake

CASTLE CAKE

MAKE THE FLAGS FOR THIS CAKE BY FOLDING SELF-ADHESIVE LABELS OVER COCKTAIL STICKS. DRAW WITH FELT TIP OR STICK COLOURED PAPER ON THE FLAGS TO MAKE DESIGNS.

1 × 23 cm (9 inch) square cake (see Chequered Chocolate Cake, page 61)
1½ quantities Chocolate Fudge Frosting (see page 91)
4 mini milk chocolate Swiss rolls
about 60 milk chocolate finger biscuits
2 after dinner mints
4 flags, toy soldiers and birthday candles to decorate

Slice the cake in half horizontally and spread with a thin layer of chocolate fudge frosting. Replace the top half and cover the cake with the remaining frosting. Mark lines across the top with a fork, first in one direction then at right angles.

Place the cake on a square cake board. Place the mini chocolate Swiss rolls on end at each corner to make turrets. Press chocolate fingers up the sides of the cake (trimming them to size, if necessary). Leave a space for the door on one side. Make the door from an after dinner mint and 2 chocolate fingers placed so that they are in line with the other biscuits. Place the other after dinner mint flat on the board in front of the door to make a drawbridge.

Decorate with flags, soldiers and birthday candles.

MAKES 18-20 PIECES

Nutritional content per serving: Carbohydrate: 61 g   Fat: 19 g   Fibre: 2 g   Kilocalories: 420

WICKED COCONUT MALLOWS

desiccated coconut
40 g (1½ oz) butter
2 tablespoons milk
250 g (8 oz) Devon toffees
75 g (3 oz) plain chocolate, broken
125 g (4 oz) icing sugar, sifted
125 g (4 oz) marshmallows, chopped
50 g (2 oz) unsalted peanuts

Generously sprinkle 2 sheets of greaseproof paper with desiccated coconut. Mix the butter, milk, toffees and chocolate in a heatproof bowl, then place over a saucepan of gently simmering water. Stir until melted, then remove from the heat and stir in the icing sugar, marshmallows and peanuts. Tip half the mixture on to each prepared sheet of greaseproof paper so that each forms a rough rectangle. Using the paper roll each into a sausage shape about 3.5 cm (1½ inches) in diameter. They should be well covered with coconut.

Wrap in foil and refrigerate for 2 hours, then cut into slices. Cover and refrigerate until required.

MAKES 50-60

Nutritional content per serving: Carbohydrate: 9 g   Fat: 2 g   Kilocalories: 58

GRANDFATHER CLOCK

300 g (10 oz) butter, softened
300 g (10 oz) caster sugar
5 eggs
250 g (8 oz) self-raising flour
50 g (2 oz) cocoa powder
2 tablespoons milk
5 drops vanilla flavouring
TO DECORATE:
2½ quantities Chocolate Buttercream Icing
  (see page 91)
½ quantity Chocolate Glacé Icing (see
  page 91) using only 2 teaspoons water
liquorice strips
3 round liquorice allsorts
chocolate mice

Make the sponge, following the instructions for Chocolate Buttercream Sponge (see page 68) but using the ingredients in quantities given here.

Grease and line the base of 2 × 18 cm (7 inch) sandwich tins and 1 × 18 cm (7 inch) shallow square tin and divide the cake mixture between them. Level the mixture in each tin and bake in a preheated oven, 190°C, 375°F, Gas Mark 5 for 20 minutes or until risen and an inserted skewer comes out clean. Leave in the tins for 5 minutes, then transfer to wire racks to cool.

Cut the square cake in half vertically and sandwich together with a little buttercream to form the clock case. Sandwich the round cakes together with buttercream to form the clock face.

Line a rectangular board with foil and position the clock face and clock case. Spread the top and sides of the cake evenly with buttercream. Spoon the remaining buttercream into a piping bag fitted with a small fluted nozzle and pipe small stars around the clock face and as a border to the clock case. Mark the numerals carefully on the clock face using a skewer. Place the thick glacé icing in a piping bag fitted with a fine lettering nozzle and pipe the numerals on to the clock face.

Cut the liquorice strips for clock hands, and use 2 more strips to make a pendulum. Place 1 liquorice allsort in the centre of the hands and use others as pendulum weights. Arrange the mice.

MAKES 18-20 PIECES

Nutritional content per serving: Carbohydrate: 69 g   Fat: 31 g   Fibre: 0.5 g   Kilocalories: 560

TRUFFLES

50 g (2 oz) trifle sponges
175 g (6 oz) plain chocolate, melted
50 g (2 oz) butter, melted
1 tablespoon brandy or rum
2 egg yolks, beaten
50 g (2 oz) icing sugar, sifted
chocolate sugar strands or cocoa powder
to coat

Make the trifle sponges into fine crumbs by placing them in a blender or food processor, or by rubbing between the fingertips. Set aside.

In a bowl, mix together the melted chocolate, butter, brandy or rum and egg yolks. Stir in the reserved crumbs with the icing sugar, then mix well. Place the mixture in the refrigerator for about 30 minutes or until firm enough to handle.

Roll teaspoonfuls of the mixture into balls in the palm of the hand. Toss each truffle in chocolate sugar strands or sifted cocoa powder and store in a covered container until required.

MAKES 35-40

Nutritional content per serving:	Carbohydrate: 5 g	Fat: 3 g	Kilocalories: 53

Wicked Coconut Mallows; Truffles; Grandfather Clock

ICINGS & SAUCES

PUT THE FINISHING TOUCHES TO YOUR GÂTEAUX, CAKES AND BISCUITS WITH ONE OF
THESE DELICIOUS CHOCOLATE ICINGS; MAKE ICE CREAMS AND DESSERTS EVEN MORE
OF A TREAT BY OCCASIONALLY SERVING THEM WITH AN EASILY MADE, BUT MOUTH-
WATERING HOT OR COLD CHOCOLATE SAUCE.

CHOCOLATE FUDGE FROSTING

50 g (2 oz) butter or margarine
25 g (1 oz) soft brown sugar
1½ tablespoons milk
50 g (2 oz) plain chocolate flavour cake
  covering, melted
175 g (6 oz) icing sugar, sifted

Place the butter or margarine in a saucepan with the sugar and milk and heat gently until dissolved. Stir in the melted chocolate, then beat in the icing sugar, mixing thoroughly.

MAKES ENOUGH TO FILL AND COVER A 15-18 CM (6-7 INCH) CAKE

Nutritional content per quantity: Carbohydrate: 243 g   Fat: 56 g   Fibre: 1 g   Kilocalories: 1435

CHOCOLATE BUTTERCREAM ICING

2 tablespoons cocoa powder
1½ tablespoons boiling water
125 g (4 oz) sunflower margarine
250 g (8 oz) icing sugar, sifted
4 drops vanilla flavouring

In a cup, mix the cocoa powder with the boiling water and set aside. Beat the margarine until creamy. Gradually add the cocoa mixture and the icing sugar. Beat well, then stir in the vanilla flavouring. To make Vanilla Buttercream Icing, omit the cocoa powder

MAKES ENOUGH TO FILL AND COVER AN 18-20 CM (7-8 INCH) CAKE

Nutritional content per quantity: Carbohydrate: 266 g   Fat: 108 g   Kilocalories: 1991

CHOCOLATE GLACÉ ICING

90 g (3½ oz) icing sugar
1 tablespoon cocoa powder
1½ tablespoons hot water

Sift the icing sugar and cocoa powder into a bowl and add the water. Mix well and use immediately. To make Plain Glacé Icing omit the cocoa powder, and use 125 g (4 oz) icing sugar instead of 90 g (3½ oz).

MAKES ENOUGH TO COVER AN 18-20 CM (7-8 INCH) CAKE

Nutritional content per quantity: Carbohydrate: 96 g   Fat: 3 g   Kilocalories: 401

CHOCOLATE MOULDED FROSTING

275 g (9 oz) icing sugar
25 g (1 oz) cocoa powder
50 g (2 oz) sunflower margarine
1 tablespoon milk
1 teaspoon vanilla flavouring

Sift together the icing sugar and cocoa powder. Combine the margarine, milk and vanilla flavouring in a heatproof bowl and place over a saucepan of gently simmering water. Heat until the margarine has melted. Remove from the heat, and beat in the icing sugar and cocoa. Allow to become cold and knead well before using.

MAKES ENOUGH TO COVER AN 18-20 CM (7-8 INCH) CAKE

Nutritional content per quantity: Carbohydrate: 292 g   Fat: 87 g   Kilocalories: 1901

Chocolate Fudge Frosting; Chocolate Buttercream Icing; Chocolate Glacé Icing; Chocolate Moulded Frosting

CHOCOLATE SAUCE

40 g (1½ oz) soft brown sugar
40 g (1½ oz) caster sugar
40 g (1½ oz) cocoa powder
150 ml (¼ pint) milk
15 g (½ oz) margarine
½ teaspoon vanilla flavouring

Gently heat the ingredients in a saucepan, stirring until the sugar dissolves. Bring to the boil and boil rapidly for 1½ minutes without stirring, until the sauce coats the back of a spoon. Serve hot or cold.

MAKES APPROXIMATELY 200 ML (7 FL OZ)

Nutritional content per quantity:	Carbohydrate: 95 g	Fat: 27 g	Kilocalories: 647

CHOCOLATE FUDGE SAUCE

125 g (4 oz) plain chocolate, broken
25 g (1 oz) soft brown sugar
½ teaspoon instant coffee granules
1 × 170 g (6 oz) can evaporated milk
2 drops vanilla flavouring

Place all the ingredients in a saucepan and heat gently until the chocolate has melted and the sugar dissolved. Bring to the boil, lower the heat and simmer uncovered for 3 minutes. Serve warm or cold.

MAKES APPROXIMATELY 300 ML (½ PINT)

Nutritional content per quantity:	Carbohydrate: 127 g	Fat: 52 g	Fibre: 2 g	Kilocalories: 1025

CHOCOLATE CUSTARD SAUCE

1 tablespoon cornflour
1 teaspoon cocoa powder
1 tablespoon caster sugar
300 ml (½ pint) milk
50 g (2 oz) plain chocolate, grated or
    chopped
½ teaspoon vanilla flavouring

In a bowl, mix the cornflour, cocoa powder and sugar to a paste with a little of the milk. Place the remaining milk in a saucepan and add the chocolate. Heat slowly until the chocolate has melted and the milk is coming to the boil. Pour on to the cornflour mixture, stirring. Return to the pan and heat, stirring, until the sauce comes to the boil and thickens. Add the vanilla and simmer for 2 minutes, stirring. Serve the sauce hot.

MAKES APPROXIMATELY 300 ML (½ PINT)

Nutritional content per quantity:	Carbohydrate: 77 g	Fat: 27 g	Fibre: 1 g	Kilocalories: 585

QUICK CHOCOLATE SAUCE

125 g (4 oz) plain chocolate, broken
3 tablespoons golden syrup
25 g (1 oz) unsalted butter

Combine the chocolate and syrup in a bowl and place over a pan of simmering water. Stir occasionally until the chocolate has melted. Add the butter and beat until smooth. Use immediately.

MAKES APPROXIMATELY 150 ML (¼ PINT)

Nutritional content per quantity:	Carbohydrate: 117 g	Fat: 57 g	Fibre: 2 g	Kilocalories: 975

Chocolate Sauce; Chocolate Fudge Sauce; Chocolate Custard Sauce; Quick Chocolate Sauce

CHOCOLATE MINT SAUCE

175 g (6 oz) plain chocolate, broken
284 ml (10 fl oz) single cream
50 g (2 oz) caster sugar
1 teaspoon peppermint flavouring

Place all the ingredients, except the peppermint flavouring, into a saucepan and heat gently until the chocolate has melted and the sugar has dissolved. Bring to the boil, lower the heat and simmer uncovered for 2 minutes, then stir in the peppermint flavouring. Serve hot or cold.

MAKES APPROXIMATELY 450 ML (¾ PINT)

Nutritional content per quantity: Carbohydrate: 175 g   Fat: 111 g   Kilocalories: 1718

CHOCOLATE RUM SAUCE

300 ml (½ pint) double cream
1 tablespoon rum
250 g (8 oz) plain chocolate, broken

Pour the cream and rum into a pan and gradually bring to the boil. Add the chocolate and stir until it has melted and the sauce is smooth. Serve hot or cold.

MAKES APPROXIMATELY 450 ML (¾ PINT)

Nutritional content per quantity: Carbohydrate: 168 g   Fat: 218 g   Kilocalories: 2687

MOCHA SAUCE

1 teaspoon instant coffee powder
150 ml (¼ pint) warm water
175 g (6 oz) plain chocolate, broken
50 g (2 oz) caster sugar

Dissolve the coffee powder in the warm water and pour into a saucepan with the remaining ingredients. Heat gently until the sugar has dissolved. Bring to the boil, lower the heat and simmer gently, uncovered for 10 minutes. Serve hot or cold.

MAKES APPROXIMATELY 300 ML (½ PINT)

Nutritional content per quantity: Fat: 51 g   Kilocalories: 1118

CHOCOLATE ORANGE SAUCE

125 g (4 oz) plain chocolate, broken
finely grated rind and juice of 1 orange
1 × 170 g (6 oz) can evaporated milk
2 tablespoons Cointreau or other orange liqueur

Place all the ingredients, except the liqueur, into a saucepan and heat gently until the chocolate has melted. Bring to the boil, lower the heat and simmer uncovered for 3 minutes, then add the liqueur. Serve warm or cold.

MAKES APPROXIMATELY 450 ML (¾ PINT)

Nutritional content per quantity: Carbohydrate: 121 g   Fat: 52 g   Kilocalories: 1068

Chocolate Mint Sauce; Mocha Sauce; Chocolate Rum Sauce; Chocolate Orange Sauce

INDEX